ESSAYS AND STUDIES
1972

Professor Beatrice White

ESSAYS AND STUDIES
1972

IN HONOUR OF BEATRICE WHITE

BEING VOLUME TWENTY-FIVE OF THE NEW SERIES
OF ESSAYS AND STUDIES COLLECTED FOR
THE ENGLISH ASSOCIATION

BY T. S. DORSCH

JOHN MURRAY

FIFTY ALBEMARLE STREET LONDON

© The English Association 1972

Printed in Great Britain by
Cox & Wyman, Ltd, London, Fakenham and Reading

0 7195 2696 5

Contents

Preface: Beatrice White

FOR the first time in its sixty-three years as an annual publication *Essays and Studies* is appearing as a *Festschrift*, and this is one measure of the esteem and affection in which Beatrice White is held by her friends and colleagues in the English Association. She has for many years been a very prominent figure in the Association—as a member of its Executive and Publications committees, as co-editor for four and editor for ten years of *The Year's Work in English Studies*, as collector of one issue of *Essays and Studies* and contributor to four other issues, as a lecturer on a number of occasions, and for the past two years as a Trustee. But the English Association is only one of many societies in which she has been active. She is a Fellow of the Royal Society of Literature, of the Royal Historical Society, and of the Society of Antiquaries, and a member of, among others, the Philological Society, the Viking Society, and the Folklore Society. She has lectured before these and other learned societies; at a number of English, American, and German universities; and at the Conference of University Professors of English held in Paris in 1953; and she enjoys the distinction of being the only woman to have lectured to the Medieval Academy of America, at Harvard University.

Such a catalogue as this can do no more than provide evidence of the wide range of interests of an unusually versatile scholar. The depth of her scholarship is attested by the very impressive list of her writings which appears at the end of this volume. About her eminence in her chosen fields of medieval and Renaissance studies there can be no dispute. But most of those who know her will think of her above all as an inspiring teacher, as a most stimulating and amusing companion, and as a staunch and generous friend.

After a distinguished student career in England and America, Beatrice White devoted herself for some years to editorial work for the Early English Text Society and the Shakespeare Association, and then became a Lecturer in English at Queen Mary College, in the University of London. The last thirty years of her academic career were given to Westfield College, where she was in turn Lecturer, Reader, and, by conferment of title, Professor of English Language and Literature. She is now Professor Emeritus of the University of London. It is especially in her setting at Westfield that she will be remembered. Many hundreds of students and of older friends—most people that she meets seem to become her friends—will recall the delightful parties that she gave in her rooms there, rooms which, crammed with books and with paintings (some by herself), and crowded with the gifts of friends and with the plants and flowers and shells and other pretty objects with which she loves to surround herself, so vividly reflected her personality. These parties were enlivened not only by the witty conversations or vigorous discussions that she has such a talent for inaugurating, but often by music—supplied perhaps by herself at the piano, perhaps by an Indian student with an exotic stringed instrument, perhaps by voices united in not necessarily reverent song. It was not only in her private capacity that she shone as a hostess; during her period as Vice-Principal she enhanced the long-standing reputation of the college for hospitality, and in her various terms as acting head of the Department of English she likewise demonstrated that the burdens of office may be carried with elegance as well as with authority. She has been unfailingly generous in sharing her scholarship with others, and numerous of her colleagues, myself among them, have been grateful to her for facilitating the publication of their work, and in many other ways helping them to use such talents as they possess.

But of course Beatrice White's life has not been confined to Westfield, or to London, or to England. She has travelled widely, both at the dictate of her curiosity and her thirst for new experience, and in response to invitations to visit foreign universities. She has friends and admirers in innumerable places of learning—learning in the sciences and the arts as well as in literature—on both sides of the Atlantic. In the summer of 1971 I attended conferences at the Universities of British Columbia and of Istanbul. At both Beatrice White was the person about whose welfare I was most frequently asked, and about whom I was most frequently able to exchange reminiscences. Many of her friends will be disappointed at not having had an opportunity of contributing to this little volume. However, within the limitations necessarily imposed on a collector of *Essays and Studies*, I have merely been able to suggest, by my choice of papers, the international character of her friendships, and the wide span, in time and topic, of her scholarly preoccupations. It would have needed a *Festschrift* of considerable size adequately to represent her extensive interests. The few must stand for the very many who would have wished to pay an affectionate tribute to Beatrice White in a volume published in her honour.

T. S. D.

Dame Trot and her Progeny

C. H. TALBOT

In 1059, according to Ordericus Vitalis, Raoul Malacorona made a journey through Italy visiting all the famous schools and centres of learning. He was proud of his own intellectual attainments and found great satisfaction in comparing his achievements with those of his Italian rivals. Besides his competence in the arts and his skill in dialectic he possessed exceptional experience in medicine and surgery, and his complacency on this score was not ruffled until he reached Salerno, where for the first time he met a woman whose medical knowledge equalled his own.

On the basis of this episode it has been suggested that already in the middle of the eleventh century there were women doctors at Salerno and that Trotula, Chaucer's Dame Trot, was one of them. The existence of a treatise *De Passionibus Mulierum* dealing with cosmetics, the troubles of pregnancy, difficult labour, birth, and so on, attributed to Trotula, would appear to confirm this view, though perhaps it reflects no more than the practice of midwifery. In this connection the translation of Malacorona's *sapientem matronam* might be emended from the usual 'wise woman' to 'sage-femme', providing a more correct assessment of the medical knowledge possessed by the Salernitan women.

On the other hand the treatises of the professional physicians of Salerno contain many references to the remedies employed by women in the cure of various diseases. In one of the most popular medical books of the Middle Ages, the *Circa Instans* of Matthew Platearius, there are no fewer than fourteen recipes attributed to the women of Salerno, and though a number of these are concerned with beauty treatment (cleansing the skin, dyeing and softening the hair, etc.), some of them deal with abdominal pains, pleurisy, haemorrhoids, and various female ailments. Bernard of

Provence also recommended such remedies, as did the compiler of the *De aegritudinum curatione*, the standard medical text employed in the schools of Salerno.

There is evidence, then, that women had some medical learning and practice in the eleventh and twelfth centuries, but whether this entitles them to be called lady doctors is another matter. Nowhere in the texts is the name 'physician' or 'surgeon' applied to them. They are simply called *Mulieres Salernitanae*.

The presumption that these women were merely medical practitioners and not truly doctors is based on their exclusion from the universities and other centres of learning. Though the school at Salerno was essentially a lay institution under the jurisdiction of the secular power, women had no place there and consequently they had no access to scientific training which would enable them to compete with the men who attended lectures, took degrees, and obtained the requisite licence to practise. Though women's intrusion into the medical profession was tolerated, it was not welcomed, and it seems quite clear that it was restricted to the fields of gynaecology and paediatrics, in which medical men showed no interest.

In Paris, where the University was administered by the ecclesiastical authorities, the exclusion of women from the practice of medicine was total. At the beginning the study of medicine had been grudgingly accepted as a branch of the arts, and it was not till the second half of the thirteenth century that it attained the status of an independent Faculty. But when it did so, it immediately claimed papal and royal privileges, and on the strength of these arrogated to itself the complete monopoly of medical practice. It was therefore impossible for anyone who lacked a degree and licence from the Faculty to treat the sick on a professional basis. Those who attempted it were faced with the severest penalties, and were either banished or thrown into prison.

In spite of this, women practitioners continued to flourish. One of the earliest of these in France was Hersende. That she received recognition was due perhaps to the fact that the Faculty of Medicine had not yet assumed its full powers and she enjoyed royal protection. She was in the service of King Louis IX of France as physician and surgeon, accompanying him to the Holy Land on the Crusade of 1248. She followed him throughout the first part of the campaign, and only after Louis' defeat, capture, eventual ransom, and return to Acre did she decide to go back to France. She married the king's apothecary and was still alive and practising in Paris nine years later, when she bought a house on the Petit Pont.

We hear of another woman doctor at Lyons in 1265, Stephanie de Montaeis, who had taken over her father's practice when he died. This suggests that she had learned her profession from him and had passed through some kind of apprenticeship, such as the Jews established. Jews, like women, were excluded from the universities, but this did not prevent them from becoming the most competent doctors of the times or from being employed by hospitals, noblemen, high ecclesiastics, or by the Pope himself. The only way they could learn their medicine was from books or from their fathers, but they succeeded in establishing dynasties of physicians which covered several generations. As a result, Jewesses were prominent in the medical profession. One of them, Sarah of Saint-Gilles, even set up as a teacher. Whilst she was practising at Marseilles, she drew up a contract in 1326 with a certain Salves de Burgonovo, promising to teach him everything she knew about medicine and the natural sciences, and engaging herself to feed, clothe, and house him until he had finished his apprenticeship. On his side Salves bound himself to give her all the money he earned by the practice of medicine during that time.

Many other instances could be cited both from France and Italy, particularly from Florence, to show that women not only studied medicine and taught it, but also treated patients. But their path was not smooth, as the following case proves.

On Wednesday, August 11, 1322, the Faculty of Medicine at Paris brought a suit against Jacqueline Felicie, saying that many years before a decree had been issued forbidding anyone who did not possess the requisite degrees from the Faculty to practise medicine under pain of excommunication and a fine of sixty pounds. And since Jacqueline had not studied at the University and had not been approved by the Faculty, she was liable to both these penalties. She was therefore summoned to the Court for sentence. In the following October witnesses were called against her, and the points on which the judges wished to be satisfied were the following:

1 That she had practised in Paris and the suburbs, visiting the sick, examining their urine, taking their pulse, and feeling their bodies and members.
2 That she had asserted she would cure them and had made a contract to do so and had received money from them.
3 That having drawn up the contract for curing their diseases, wounds, abscesses, etc., she had visited them in their homes and treated them *ad modum physicorum et medicorum*.
4 That she gave them syrups to drink and other strengthening, laxative, and digestive medicines, either liquid, solid, or aromatic, which they drank in her presence and under her instructions.
5 That in spite of the fact that she was not approved by the Faculty of Medicine nor by the Chancellor of the Cathedral of Paris, she had practised medicine and continued to do so from day to day.
6 That she had done this even after being warned by the Faculty.

The first witness was John of St. Omer, a taverner and citizen of Paris. He said that he had been ill on the feast of St. John the Baptist (June 24), and that Jacqueline had visited him many times and been so solicitous about him that without her he was convinced that he would never have been cured. He had made a contract with her in the presence of his wife and John the Smith, the compact being that no payment should be given unless there were a cure. The sum agreed on was forty shillings. This he paid. Asked what disease he suffered from, he said he did not know, but thought there were several. Jacqueline had given him a clear liquid to drink after she had drunk some herself to show that it was harmless, and it had cured him. Asked whether he spoke out of friendship or hatred for her, he said on his oath that he wished only to speak the truth.

John the Smith was the next witness. He said he had suffered a great deal in his head and ears during the excessive heat of the summer. Jacqueline visited him, gave him some medicines to drink, one of which was green, the others clear. He had not made any contract, but when he was cured, he gave her a sum of money quite voluntarily.

Odo of Cormicy, one of the brothers serving at the Hotel Dieu in Paris, was the next witness. He had been suffering from some infirmity which prevented him from standing up. He had been visited by John of the Tower and several other Masters of Medicine of the Faculty, namely Master Martin, Master Hermann, and others, all without success. So he had himself taken to Jacqueline's house, where he stayed for a while before being taken back to the hospital again. Jacqueline visited him there, gave him baths, smeared him with ointments, gave him herbs like camomile, melilot, and others which he could not remember. On the instructions of Jacqueline a fire was prepared, a bed of herbs placed on top, and when the herbs had burned, she placed him on the ashes, causing a great sweat. Then he was wrapped in a sheet and put to bed, where he recovered his health and strength. Asked whether he had made a contract with her, he said no; but of his own free will he gave her some money when he was better. He had heard that she was more experienced in surgery and medicine than any Master of Medicine or Surgery living in Paris.

The next witness was Clemence of Beauvais, a potter, who lived opposite the royal palace. Whilst she was in the hands of the doctors, who could do nothing for her, her husband heard about the cures effected by Jacqueline and sent for her. Jacqueline examined her urine, took her pulse, but said nothing. She then gave her a medicine to drink made of herbs, but the taste was so horrible that she could not swallow it, and so both her husband and her doctors forbade her to drink it.

Jeanne Bilbaut then gave evidence that she had been suffering from a fever on the feast of St. Christopher (July 25), and she was treated by many physicians, namely a friar, Master Hermann,

Master Manfred of Milan, and many others. She was so ill on July 25 that she could not speak, and the doctors had decided that she would die (*phisicique predicti eam judicabant ad mortem*). And so it would have been, if Jacqueline had not come to her aid. Jacqueline examined her urine, took her pulse, gave her something to drink, and then prescribed a certain syrup which made her go to the lavatory. But she got well. Asked whether she had made a contract, she said no, and that after her recovery Jacqueline had refused the money she offered.

Jeanne de Moncy, a widow, said she suffered from an intestinal complaint for which she had been in hospital at St. Sulpice for eleven days, being visited and treated there by Masters Gilbert, Hermann, Manfred, and Thomas, all doctors of the Faculty, who could do nothing for her. When she realized this, she sent for Jacqueline, who eventually cured her, refusing to take any remuneration. Asked if she knew whether Jacqueline visited and treated other patients, she said she had heard so, and she knew that Jacqueline had cured the Royal Chancellor of gout, his nephew who was unable to walk, and many others, whose names she did not know.

Another witness, Matilda, wife of John of St. Omer, the taverner, said that she had been ill from the middle of Lent (March 17) until June 24, and during that time she had been treated by many doctors, who could do nothing for her. So she sent for Jacqueline, who cured her within twelve days. Jacqueline had given her certain drinks, and put plasters and fomentations on her chest. No contract had been made, but when the cure was established, she had paid a certain sum.

The last witness, Yvo Tuelue, was a serving man at the Royal Court in Paris. He had been sick with a continuous fever and many doctors had treated him without success. Yvo had sent for Jacqueline, and she had cured him with medicines, *quod facere non potuerunt medici, qui eum visitabant.*

So, though all these witnesses had been called to give testimony against her, not one complained of the results obtained. No other witness was asked to give evidence, and it is interesting to note that the Faculty failed to find anyone who would support its case.

On November 2, 1322, Jacqueline was summoned to Court by the Faculty to answer her judges. They heard more than they had bargained for. Jacqueline, it appears, was not a back-street practitioner, a charlatan, or an ignoramus. She was a noblewoman, who had to be addressed as *Domina*.

She immediately launched an attack on the legality of the Court. She declared that she was not bound to make any statement unless the Masters of the Faculty gave proof of their jurisdiction and of the commission granted to them, a copy of which should be provided for her.

Secondly, she was not bound to answer John of St. Nicholas, who claimed to be acting as proctor for the Dean and Masters, until he gave proof of his mandate.

Thirdly, if any statute, decree, admonition, prohibition, or excommunication had been published by the Faculty, it applied to simple, ignorant people who practised medicine, and not to her, because she was an expert in medicine, well instructed in the rules of the medical art.

Furthermore, the said statute, decree, admonition, etc., had been aimed at unlawful and ignorant practitioners in Paris 102 years ago, and now they were all dead. Jacqueline was not even born then, nor for a good sixty years afterwards, since she was only in her thirties now, as appeared by her face. In the statute and decree everything was couched in the past tense and applied to conditions a hundred years back, and not to the present day, when she was being summoned. So no faith could be placed in such documents.

The law says that what concerns everybody should be approved by everybody. But in this statute there is no mention of doctors of the Faculty, bachelors, scholars, nor of the bishop, archbishop, lords, barons, citizens and the people of Paris, whose interest is at stake. Not one of them is named in the statute. And since these people are neither named in the statute nor called to give evidence, the statute and decree are null and void and do not affect her.

Furthermore, it is better for a woman, wise and expert in

B

medicine, to treat women patients, especially in sexual matters, rather than a man, who is not allowed to touch a woman's hands, breast, abdomen, feet, legs, etc.: indeed, a man ought to avoid dealing with the secret parts of a woman. For it has happened that women would rather die than allow a man to examine them, and this is a well-known fact, of which the Dean and Masters of the Faculty are well aware.

And even supposing, without prejudice to her case, that it is wrong for a woman to treat the sick and examine them, it is less wrong for a woman, who is expert in medicine, to do so, because patients of both sexes, who are afraid of revealing their secrets to a man, do not want to die. The law says that minor evils should be tolerated in order to avoid greater ones. And as Jacqueline is an expert in the art of medicine, it is better that she should be allowed to treat patients than that they should die. Indeed, far from allowing them to die, she has cured many.

It has been found and proved that many patients of both sexes, suffering from grave diseases, have been treated by Masters of the Faculty and have not been cured. On the contrary, when Jacqueline was called in afterwards, she was able to heal them within a short time.

The statute and decree which sentence her to excommunication and a fine of sixty pounds are null and void, for any admonition or prohibition made by an ecclesiastical court is invalid if it carries with it a monetary penalty.

The law also says that officials of ecclesiastical courts cannot take cognizance of crimes or punish them without the authority, personally granted to the officials, of the person holding jurisdiction. But in the official's letters there is no mention of his having been commissioned by the Bishop and given power to punish.

Furthermore, any statute which infringes public interest automatically becomes invalid by law. The statute and decree which the Masters of the Faculty have published are contrary to the public interest, which is the healing of the sick. This Jacqueline has done.

The law also presumes that anyone exercising a craft or profession is a good person and acting well until the opposite is proved. The law is therefore on her side, because she exercises the art of medicine well by curing her patients, and it presumes she understands the art of healing. So the statute affects only ignorant practitioners, who ply their craft badly. It does not apply to Jacqueline.

For these and other reasons the sentence of the Dean and Faculty is without effect, and should not hinder her practice of medicine.

Moreover, because she has been put to great trouble and vexation, she claims legitimate costs from the prosecutors.

One might have thought that such a spirited defence would have put the judges to shame. But they were adamant. And in order to prove their case they resorted to the most diverse, one might say perverse, arguments.

The Faculty said that the statute which had been invoked against her had been approved by the officials of the Court and the kings of France for the past sixty years. Jacqueline was completely ignorant of the art of medicine and was not literate, nor had she been approved by the Faculty, nor could she explain the causes and reasons of the said art of medicine.

Also it is forbidden in law for a woman to be an advocate and a witness in a criminal case. (They had evidently forgotten that they had called female witnesses for themselves.)

Furthermore, it is more dangerous to kill a man through giving him the wrong medicines and enemas than it is to lose a case in court through the ignorance and lack of skill of lawyers. And since the killing of a man is a mortal sin, and sin pertains to the ecclesiastical sphere, the sentence is valid and binds the defendant. (What reasoning!)

As to the claim that it is better for a woman to treat women's complaints, it is not worthy of reply.

On the plea that she ought to be allowed to practise in order to avoid a greater evil, this should be rejected, because the defendant is ignorant of medicine and she has not attended lectures in the schools as she ought to have done.

As for the argument that she has cured many patients whom the Masters of the Faculty failed to cure, such a reason is frivolous, because it is certain that a Master of Medicine who has been approved by the Faculty can cure patients more surely than a woman can.

So the Faculty won its case and presumably, though there are no documents to prove it, Jacqueline was excommunicated. What effect this would have on her we find out from another prosecution, where a woman named Clarissa of Rouen was sentenced by the conservator of the privileges of the University for the same offence. It forbade anyone to walk, return, stand, sit, eat, or drink with her, or to furnish food or drink, water or fire, or the use of an oven or mill. No one was allowed even to proffer help or advice, or to buy or sell any commodity such as bread and wine, fish and meat, clothes and footwear. In fact it made her a complete outcast. In this particular case, however, Clarissa and her husband appealed from the official in Paris to her own Bishop of Rouen, a move that exasperated him, because he was afraid that the Faculty would be drawn to another Court where its legal expenses would be increased.

The number of prosecutions for what the Faculty called 'illegal practice' mounted as the years went by, but the flow of women practitioners continued unabated. We find them at Dijon, Lyons, Rheims, Beauvais, Douai, in fact, everywhere. Some of them became barber-surgeons and attended the hospitals, others like Marguerite, who received six shillings from the Countess of Artois 'pour garir le petit Pieret de sa teste', were accepted into the houses of the rich. But the threat of dire penalties always hung over them and some were expelled from towns, others thrown into prison, some even burned for heresy and witchcraft.

Whilst this was going on in Paris, the exact opposite was happening under the Angevins in Spain and the south of Italy. One of the reasons was that the universities and the medical faculties were not under ecclesiastical control, but under government jurisdiction. The appointing of lawyers, professors of medicine and so on was in the hands of the king, and therefore the attitude was altogether more liberal. Provided a person could pass the test of competence in any professional capacity, that person could obtain a licence from the king to practise his or her art.

And so we have records covering more than a century in which women are shown as practising doctors and surgeons.

What happened in these cases was this. A woman would learn all about some branch of medicine or surgery from her father or perhaps a close relative. She would then get a testimonial letter from the town or district in which she lived saying that she was of good morals, a practising Christian, expert at her job, and a good servant of the Crown. With this testimonial she would present herself at the Court in Naples and be examined by two royal physicians or surgeons. If found competent she would be granted a licence to practise, the exact limits of her treatment being described and the region where she could work being defined.

The earliest of these records goes back to 1307, when a certain Francesca was examined and found expert in the art of surgery and able to cure and treat patients. In the same year another woman named Trotta (note the name) was examined by Raynald the Royal Surgeon and found expert in the cure of various sicknesses, wounds, ulcers, and external abscesses. Her licence was granted for treating these conditions.

Two years later Maria Gallicia was examined and found expert in the art of surgery, particularly in the cure of wounds, abscesses, ruptures, diseases of the womb, and other feminine ailments. She was licensed to practise in the whole kingdom of Naples.

Some doubt may be expressed as to whether the examinations of these women was rigid enough in view of their supposed lack of education. Well, Lauretta, in 1309, was examined by Francesco da Piedmonte, who had been a lecturer at the University of Bologna, was now professor at Naples, and had written a treatise on practical medicine which applied the theories of both Arab and Salternitan medicine. He found that she was competent to cure various diseases, abscesses, external wounds, but what is most important, to operate for stone, a most complicated and dangerous operation. All the same, the examiner had to remark that she was *ydiota*, that is, she knew only her native language and was therefore unable to read the Latin texts of medicine on which the university medical course was based.

Let us see one of these royal licences, issued by King Charles and addressed to his justices:

> In all our actions we publicly, willingly and carefully look to the public good and try to preserve public morals. Now Francesca, the wife of Matthew de Romano, who comes from Salerno, has stated in our Royal Court that she is competent to carry out the principal duties of surgery, and according to the judgement of others has a reputation in such matters. Wherefore she has begged our Excellency to grant her a licence to practise this art. And because a public testimonial from the whole territory of Salerno has been presented to this royal court showing that the aforesaid Francesca is a practising christian, she has been examined by our royal physicians and surgeons in the art of surgery, and though she knows no Latin, she has been found competent. And although it is not seemly for women to be in the company of men, lest their modesty be put to shame and they incur the penalty of transgression against the law, nevertheless taking into consideration that women are better suited to treating sick women and their ailments than men are and morals are better preserved, we grant her licence to cure and practise this art in your territory, having received from her the usual oath that she will treat patients according to the traditions of the same art. Wherefore we command you, the Justices, to allow the said Francesca to practise her profession freely to our honour and the usefulness of the people, placing no obstacle or impediment in her way.

All the royal licences are couched in this manner. But in each one the exact branches of surgery in which the woman can practise are defined. So, for instance, Clarice from Foggia is licensed for women's diseases and for diseases of the eyes; Sibyl from Benevento for buboes, that is, the abscesses which appear under the armpits or the groin as a result of plague or epidemic; Margharita of Naples for dangerous abscesses, perhaps cancer, of the breast and disorders of the womb; Margharita from Bitonto for

deep wounds and fistulas; Raymunda of Taberna for treating can-
kers, simple wounds, and fistulas.

In this latter case, we get an idea of the social standing of some of
these women. This is most important, because in other countries
where prohibition was made against women, the university
authorities, and particularly the medical faculties, were always at
pains to stress that women practitioners were ignorant, or old
(*quaedam vetula* is the usual term), and came from the lower classes
of society. In Raymunda's case, we find that she was the sister of
the notary in the city of San Marco. At that time notaries were
people of some standing and were usually the principal lawyers in
a town.

We must not allow ourselves, however, to be carried away
with this list of women doctors. In a period of thirty-five years
in the kingdom of Naples and Sicily there were eighteen recorded
licences given to women. But in the same period and in the same
territory there were about three thousand men. Moreover, all the
women were surgeons. Not one of them was called a physician,
and this was natural, since you could be a physician only if you
had a medical degree from the University, from which women
were barred.

However, there is one instance of a woman being called a Doctor of Medicine of the University of Naples, though I myself have
not seen the document, because so far it has not been published.
This lady was Constanza Calenda, the daughter of a famous
medical professor, who married into a noble family at the beginning of the fifteenth century.

Elsewhere the prohibition against women meddling in medicine
was upheld. In Vienna the Faculty of Medicine was particularly
hard on women practitioners. It is quite clear from the accounts of
the Faculty that nuns were practising medicine and that many
patients went to them to be cured of their ills. The Faculty pro-
tested to the Bishop of Passau and obtained an injunction against
them. The same arguments were always used, namely that since
they had not studied at the approved medical centre they could
not know any medicine. In 1469 an old woman was brought
before the Faculty, '*que indocta et certe inexperta*', because she was

treating patients. They threatened her with excommunication if she did not desist, and she was ordered to appear before the bishop's official. She did not turn up. But a year later she appeared, saying that she had been on a pilgrimage to Rome to get herself absolved from the excommunication, but that she was unable to do so without the agreement of the official at Vienna. They got her to confess that she had practised medicine 'having been deceived by the devil', and then agreed to free her from excommunication if she would have a public document drawn up at her own expense stating that she had erred and that she had defamed the Faculty. This document was to be read out publicly at the churches of Vienna, Klosterneuberg, Tuln, Melk, and St. Polten, in fact in the whole district where she was known as a medical practitioner. She was also bound to promise that she would never practise again. And since she had sinned publicly, she was also to carry out a public penance by standing for an hour in the cemetery on a raised block of stone during one of the public feast days, so that all the people passing by should recognize that they also had erred in going to her for medicine.

The lady had the last laugh. After she had been absolved and done her penance, she told the officials that she had no money to pay for the public document which had been drawn up, and resolutely refused to meet any further expenses.

By the end of the fifteenth century the condition of women practitioners had not changed, though when syphilis, brought from America by the Spaniards, and spread by the troops during the siege of Naples, became rampant, the authorities were only too glad to avail themselves of their services. At Lectoure, where special wards at the hospital were put at the disposal of those suffering from this disease, it would appear that two women were put in charge, Margot, 'a healer', and Comarenga.

Dame Trot, therefore, was not an isolated case. She had many illustrious daughters, whose services were always in great demand, particularly amongst the poor who could not afford the enormous fees demanded by the accredited physicians and surgeons. But their passage was rough, fraught with immense peril, and not always safely completed.

II

Polynices and Gunnlaug Serpent-Tongue: A Parallel

MARGARET SCHLAUCH

THE story of the fratricidal struggle between the two sons of Oedipus, Eteocles and Polynices, was transmitted to the Middle Ages by Statius (first century A.D.). His epic the *Thebaid*, a poem replete with artificial devices such as lengthy exclamations, argumentative speeches and recondite mythological allusions, must have been a delight for students and practitioners of rhetoric in the schools. As is well known, the two brothers both claimed the heritage of Thebes after their father's death; a compromise was reached in the form of an agreement that they should rule alternately, each one to spend a year on the throne while the other went into temporary exile. Eteocles was the one to rule first, but at the end of his term he refused to give up the royal office. Polynices thereupon challenged him and with the aid of his father-in-law Adrastus laid siege to the city. This is the motivation leading to the ultimate duel which resulted in the deaths of both of them.[1]

That duel is prefaced by pleading discourses from Jocasta (still alive) and Antigone, addressed to the two rivals from the city wall; also by a futile *suasoria* spoken by Adrastus. The combat is described in detail. Polynices first wounds his brother's horse and then drives his sword into the body of Eteocles. The latter fights on as long as he can remain upright, though feeble, but he falls

[1] Ancient sources differ in reporting the details of this fratricidal strife: for instance, they do not agree as to which of the two brothers was the elder, or which one ruled first before Eteocles broke the contract. See Pauly-Wissowa, *Realencyclopädie der classischen Altertumswissenschaft*, s.v. 'Polyneikes'.

down on purpose and at the last moment carries out his final deceit:

Sic pugnant miseri; restabat lassa nefando
vita duci [i.e., Eteocles] summusque cruor, poterantque
parumper stare gradus; sed sponte ruit fraudemque
supremam in media iam morte parat. (XI. 552–5)[1]

Polynices exults—prematurely, as it turns out. He approaches the prostrate Eteocles, having ordered someone to appropriate the royal insignia (*sceptrum atque insigne comarum*) while the dying man can still see. The purpose of Polynices is to take his brother's arms as well. But enough life remains in Eteocles to perform an act of vengeance. When the victor is bending over him, he summons his last strength, urged on by hatred, and plunges his sword into the heart of Polynices:

. . . . nondum ille [Eteocles] peractis
manibus ultrices animam servabat in iras.
utque superstantem pronumque in pectora sensit,
erigit occulte ferrum vitaeque labantis
reliquias tenues odio supplevit, et ensem
iam laetus fati fraterno in corde reliquit. (562–7)

Polynices still has enough breath to reproach his assailant with treachery and to threaten him with punishment at the hands of the Agenorean judge (i.e., Minos). Then he falls dead over Eteocles, and crushes him with his armed weight:

nec plura locutus
concidit et totis fratrem obruit armis. (572–3)

Although Polynices is clearly in the right about his claimed succession to the throne, his actions as a warrior are not sharply contrasted with those of Eteocles. Pity is not said to be his motive when he bends over the man he has vanquished.

[1] Quotations are taken from the edition of the *Thebaid* by J. H. Mozley in the Loeb Classical Library, 2 vols. (1928).

In the twelfth century an unknown poet[1] treated the same material in *Le Roman de Thèbes*. The narrative is freely handled with much added that is new in the way of episodes, speeches and descriptions; contemporary *mores* are often made to replace the pagan. For instance, when Parthenopeus, a champion of Polinicès, captures a horse, he sends it into the city to Antigone, whom he loves romantically, with this message:

> Por cestre enseigne mant m'amie
> Por lé ai fait chevalerie. (4371-2)

The love of King Etioclès for a Theban lady is thus described:

> Li reis ama mout Salemandre
> Celeement et senz esclandre;
> Il fu mout proz et por s'amie
> Fait mout sovent chevalerie. (9081-4)

Secrecy, avoidance of scandal and inspiration to deeds of valor—these are among the traits of a typical courtly lover.

According to the editor, L. Constans, the poet seemingly wrote without having a text of Statius before him. A full summary would have been enough, or perhaps he relied on the memory of a reading.

When he depicts the final combat of the two brothers, he introduces some very significant innovations. After the first exchange of blows, Polinicès smites Etioclès so mightily with his sword Blanchenue that the other falls down prostrate. The spectacle arouses pity in Polinicès, an emotion not attributed to the corresponding hero of Statius:

[1] About 1150, says Léopold Constans in his edition of *Le Roman*, 2 vols., SATF, No. 25 (1890). Vol. I contains the text; vol. II, introduction, commentary and notes, upon which I have relied. F. E. Guyer, *Chrétien de Troyes: Inventor of the Modern Novel* (London, 1960), proposes a date after 1167. This is part of his effort to prove that *Thèbes, Énéas and Troie* all postdate the major period of Chrétien's literary activity (c. 1150 to 1166/67). The argument is tendentious and does not seem convincing.

> Polinicès, quant iço veit,
> Que sis frère chaeiz esteit
> Et que il ert a mort feruz,
> De son cheval est descenduz;
> Tost vait a lui et veit la plaie
> Et le sanc vermeil qui fors raie. (9624–9)
>
> Pitié en ot, ne puet muer
> Que ne l'auge reconforter. (9630–1)

He embraces his brother, kissing his eyes and his face. It was an ill-fated hour, he says, when our mother bore us; at the same time he declares that it is the pride of Etioclès which caused his death ('Par vostre orgueil i estes morz,' l. 9636). The latter is both angry and dismayed. Knowing that he is doomed, and that no physician can save him, he decides on an act of felony. By a secret movement (*celeement*) he grasps his sword and gives his brother a mortal wound through the haunches. Falling to the ground (*la terre*), Polinicès utters a final reproach: I acted out of pity, he says; now you have ended our war and neither of us will possess the land:

> Dist lui: 'Frère, por quei m'as mort?
> 'Ço saches bien, fait l'as a tort:
> 'Por la pitié que oi de tei
> 'Descendi jo par bone fei;
>
> 'Or as finé ci nostre guerre,
> 'Ne jo ne tu n'avront la terre.'
> Ne puet parler: regardé l'a,
> Iluec est morz, l'anme s'en va.

It is interesting to note the emphasis on *la terre* as the incentive for action. This is true at other points as well. Early in the poem Jocasta (who does not commit suicide in this version), lamenting her widowed state, complains that in case of war she would not be able to defend the land:

> Se bataille me sort o guerre,
> Ne porrai pas tenir ma terre. (223–4)

Her situation is thus comparable to Laudine's in the *Yvain* of Chrétien de Troyes. As an issue between two brothers, *la terre* almost achieves personification. In the Arthurian romances its place might well be taken by a beautiful damsel. In folklore the treason of one brother against the other is variously motivated.[1] The combat of Eteocles and Polynices was known in Middle English by way of Lydgate's *Siege of Thebes*. In his Prologue the poet represents himself as joining Chaucer's pilgrims and contributing the lengthy account of Oedipus and his family as one of the Canterbury Tales.[2] The conclusion, which features the pacifying intervention of Theseus against Creon and on behalf of the widowed Grecian ladies, is clearly linked with the Knight's Tale. Lydgate apparently did not use the French *Roman de Thèbes* directly, but drew on a French prose version. There are two of these, namely the *Roman de Edipus* (extant in a single manuscript, F. fr. 301 of the Bibliothèque Nationale, and also in an early sixteenth-century print) and the *Ystoire de Thèbes* (published by A. Verard, 1491). There has been some discussion as to which of the two was Lydgate's immediate source,[3] but in any event he presents the final combat of the brothers in the spirit of the *Roman de Thèbes*. After Polymytes has smitten Ethyocles 'thorghout' and caused him to fall, he is touched by compassion:

> But whan he sauh/ the stremys of his blood
> Raylle about/ in maner of a flood,
> Al sodeynly/ of compassiou*n*,
> From his coursere/ he alighte dou*n*,
> And brotherly, with a pitous face,
> To saue his lyf/ gan hy*m* to vnbrace. (4279–84)

---

[1] See Stith Thompson, *Motif Index of Folk Literature* (Copenhagen, 1955–58), item K 2211.

[2] *Lydgate's Siege of Thebes*, ed. Axel Erdmann: Introduction, glossary and notes, EETS, Original Series No. 125 (1930); text, EETS, Extra Series No. 108 (1911).

[3] The debate is summarized by Alain Renoir, 'The Immediate Source of Lydgate's *Siege of Thebes*', *Studia Neophilologica*, XXXIII (1961), 86–95. The author concludes that Lydgate probably relied on a complete text of the prose *Edipus*, as suggested by Erdmann, despite discrepancies.

Moved 'of newe affeccioun', he pulls out the spear that had caused
the fatal wound, 'Of loue only/ handlyng hym ryght softe'
(4287).

> But O/ allas! whil he lay alofte,
> Ful yrously/ Ethiocles the felle,
> Of al this sorowe/ verraye sours *and* welle,
> with a dagger/ in al his peynys smerte,
> his brother smoot vnwarly to the herte:
> which al her lyf/ haddë be so wrothe. (4288–93)

Here, it will be noted, there is no final dialogue between the
brothers, and no direct reference to the reason for their feud,
namely possession of *la terre*. But Lydgate's prevailingly didactic
moral attitude is surely reflected at this point,[1] and there is no
doubt that his sympathies lie with Polymytes, shown as an
exponent of compassion.

And now for the comparable situation which appears in the
Icelandic *Gunnlaugs saga ormstungu* (thirteenth century). Here the
two protagonists, Gunnlaug and Hrafn, are not brothers or even
foster-brothers. They are both poet-warriors, who meet at the
court of the King of Sweden. At first their relationship is friendly,
but harsh rivalry develops between them as both strive to win the
favour of the King by reciting skaldic encomia of him. When
Hrafn leaves for Iceland they part as enemies. Now it happens that
Gunnlaug in his early youth had formed an attachment for a girl
named Helga, described as the loveliest woman that had ever been
in Iceland. One may discount such literary superlatives, but the
praise is nevertheless great. Helga's beauty is constantly emphasized,
yet at the same time she does not have the vigorous, even aggressive personality attributed to many other Icelandic heroines
similarly endowed by nature. Throughout the story she remains
curiously passive. Before leaving home, Gunnlaug had asked for a
formal betrothal to her, but her father—understandably cautious
in view of the candidate's belligerent temperament—had gone no

---

[1] See Robert W. Ayres, 'Medieval History, Moral Purpose, and the Structure
of Lydgate's *Siege of Thebes*', *PMLA*, LXXIII (1958), 463–74. The point about
Lydgate's general purpose is obvious, but it is worth stressing.

further than to promise that she would not be committed to anyone else for the next three years. If Gunnlaug were to return within that period, having gained a good reputation abroad, his suit might be favourably considered; if he failed to appear, Helga could be given in marriage to another candidate.

Various adventures keep Gunnlaug abroad while he is rendering military service (if such it may be called) to the kings of Sweden and Norway. He is delayed beyond the time limit agreed upon, though not very long. (It was to have been during the end of the summer of the third year.) Meantime Hrafn has presented himself as Helga's wooer, and on Gunnlaug's failure to appear, her father promptly arranges the match. Thus Gunnlaug comes home to find Helga already married.

The quarrel between the two champions flares up into a bitter duel, which however remains inconclusive. The very next day the National Assembly passes a law forbidding all such duels in the future. So Hrafn and Gunnlaug journey to Norway, each with some followers, and there the two parties join combat, somewhat like the followers of Eteocles and Polynices. All are killed except Gunnlaug and Hrafn. Gunnlaug strikes Hrafn with a mighty blow and cuts off his leg from under him. Hrafn staggers back to a tree stump and supports himself on it. The victor declares that he will no longer fight with a wounded man, yet the obdurate Hrafn wants to continue, keeping himself erect as best he can. But he needs a drink of water. Gunnlaug offers to bring it to him in his helmet, if Hrafn will not practise any deceit. This Hrafn promises. Nevertheless when Gunnlaug fetches the water from a neighbouring stream, Hrafn reaches up for it with his left hand, and with his right gives his opponent a deadly blow. Gunnlaug says, 'You have now betrayed me in evil fashion, and you behaved unmanfully when I trusted you.' Hrafn's reply is memorable. 'That is true,' he says, 'but my reason was that I begrudge you the embrace of Helga the Fair.'[1]

[1] In Icelandic: 'þá maelti Gunnlaugr: "Illa sveiktu mik nú, ok ódrengilega fór þér, þar sem ek trúða þér." Hrafn svarar: "Satt er þat," segir hann, en þat gekk mér til þess, at ek ann þér eigi faðmlagsins Helgu innar fǫgru.' Quoted from *Íslenzk Fornrit*, III, edd. Sigurður Nordal and Guðni Jónsson (Reykjavík, 1935), p. 102.

Here again we have a situation in which the deadly rivalry of two champions culminates in violent single combat; the one who first receives a mortal wound is the recipient of a generous act on the part of the other; his response is to give the benefactor a like mortal wound.

It is most unlikely that there is any source relationship between the saga and the French romanticized epic, although this is chronologically not impossible. The motivations are different: in the one case, rivalry over dynastic succession, and in the other, rivalry over a woman. Yet the kingdom of Thebes is almost personified as *la terre* (grammatically feminine), while the Helga of the saga is herself little more than a personification. The parallel may be accidental, but in any case it is interesting to notice how quite different social backgrounds can independently produce literary episodes so closely analogous in conception and execution.

III

Chaucer and the Elusion of Clarity

E. TALBOT DONALDSON

I HAVE to apologize for my title. The word *elusion* is one I was afraid I had invented—in a Joycean mood—but I subsequently found, to my relief, that it was in the *Oxford English Dictionary*. According to the *OED*, it came into being about the middle of the sixteenth century meaning 'the action of deluding or befooling a person; an illusion or deceptive appearance'. Seventy-five years later it had come also to mean 'the action of escaping dexterously from danger, pursuit, etc., of evading an argument, a command, law, or obligation'. Unable to make up its mind between 'illusion' and 'evasion', it seems to have gone into a decline, and it dropped out of the language entirely during the last century.

The reason I have revived it is that I needed a word that would accurately describe two related but distinct aspects of Chaucer's celebrated stylistic clarity. The fact is that this clarity, while it is self-evident, is often more apparent than real. It is, indeed, frequently an 'illusion or deceptive appearance' by which Chaucer 'deludes or befools a person'—namely the reader—and it is also a means by which he escapes dexterously from the danger of really being clear and from the pursuit of critics—a means by which he evades, for the sake of poetic complexity, the laws and obligations of logical simplicity. And when he uses clarity in order successfully to evade an argument, he does so by passing the argument on to his readers, who never have done with debating what that which he so clearly says actually means.

I find that what most people who read Chaucer in their school-days without really studying him remember about him are those simple declarative sentences of his, those models of straightforward discourse in which the sense is perfectly packed in a syntactical box:

C

He was a verray, parfit, gentil knight; (*CT*, A 72)[1]

or, of the Clerk:

Of studye took he most cure and most hede; (A 303)

or, of the Parson:

A bettre preest I trowe ther nowher noon is; (A 524)

or, of the Parson's brother, the Plowman:

> A trewe swinkere and a good was he,
> Living in pees and parfit charitee. (A 531–2)

Appreciation of such satisfying statements, which seem to be the direct expression of a mind that sees life steadily and sees it whole, has quite properly been one of the chief themes of Chaucerian criticism through the centuries, and, with certain critics, almost the only theme. Thus Matthew Arnold, endeavouring, I suspect, to find in Chaucer, if not high seriousness, at least that clearness and certainty of vision that Arnold's own age lacked, chose as his touchstone for Chaucer's poetry something even less than a statement, a mere apostrophe:

O martyr, souded to virginitee! (B 1769)

But Arnold's admiration for a line limited to the ideas of martyrdom, virginity, and soldering illustrates the danger of placing too great a stress on Chaucer's easy clarity; for such admiration suggests that the poet himself always saw things as all-of-a-piece, as unproblematical. Yet no great poet is unproblematical, and Chaucer as little as any. Since he is a devotee of stylistic clarity, a practitioner of the art of very logical statement, it has to be through abuse of his chief literary tool that he attains complexity

---

[1] For the text of Chaucer I have used my edition, *Chaucer's Poetry: An Anthology for the Modern Reader* (The Ronald Press, New York, 1958), but the line numbering is that of the standard editions.

—that is, through his practice of what I am calling the elusion of clarity.

Let me begin with a tiny example of this abuse, one of no real importance except in so far as it demonstrates in microcosm an habitual technique. The first three portraits of the General Prologue to the *Canterbury Tales*—the Knight, Squire, and Yeoman—are triumphs of straightforward description of genuinely worthy people who correspond in all respects to the ideals of their vocations: they're just what they should be, perfectly fitted to the simple declarative sentences that describe them. The concluding line of the series, speaking of the Yeoman, who is the least interesting and problematical of all the pilgrims, reads:

A forster was he soothly as I gesse. (A 117)

Now if one reads the line fast enough it causes only a very slight blur, which one perhaps tends to rationalize by noting that even Chaucer's Middle English sometimes seems imprecise, or, alternatively, that one's own knowledge of Middle English is imprecise. But if one pauses, the blur smudges the page: He was soothly, that is, really, truly, a forester—I guess. The statement is rather like someone picking out a plank, placing it across a stream, and then jarring it loose—all in one action. But of course the line precipitates us not into a stream but into the portrait of the Prioress, who provides a rhyme for *I gesse*—or, more probably, for whom the rhyme *I gesse* was provided.

For it is obvious that the expression 'I guess' has less to do with the Yeoman than with his describer. When one guesses parenthetically in conversational speech one does not usually mean to indicate a lack of confidence in the objective truth of one's statement; one is merely trying to prevent the listener from getting the impression that one is being dogmatic—one is enlisting his sympathy by reminding him that we all share common human fallibility. Thus 'I guess' tells us nothing at all about the Yeoman —none of us would dream of disputing the statement that he was a forester; but 'I guess' could, if we happened to hear it, remind us of the human fallibility of the narrator; and this is about to be demonstrated with a good deal of eloquence as Chaucer proceeds to unequal battle with the female charm of the Prioress, by which he is to be fondly overcome. What the seemingly clear but actually ambiguous statement about the Yeoman suggests is a shifting of gears as the poet moves from one mode of description to another —from a world where things clearly are what they seem to a world where one can only guess that things actually are what they seem, and one guess is probably as good as another.

More characteristic of Chaucer's creation of the problematical through manipulation of direct statement are his well-known juxtapositions. Such statements as those I quoted earlier about the Knight, the Clerk, and the others may be torn from their context and quoted in isolation without doing any real harm to Chaucer's sense. Beguiled by such pure simplicity, a beginning reader might easily suppose that the following statements were also absolute and in themselves complete:

> She was a worthy womman al hir live . . . A Griselda?
> Ther was nowher no man so vertuous . . . A St. Francis?

Yet, as we all know, another statement, discrete in syntax and complete in sense, often joins the first in what may seem like a shot-gun wedding:

> She was a worthy womman al hir live:
> Housbondes at chirche dore she hadde five. (A 459–60)

> Ther was nowher no man so vertuous:
> He was the beste beggere in his hous. (A 251–2)

Faced with syntactical situations like these, few editors (and I am not one of the few) can resist placing a colon after the first line, thereby warning the reader that before he allows its still fluid sense to harden in his mind he should hurry on so that it may be allowed to coalesce with the sense of the next line. I think this is legitimate editorial practice; yet it is not entirely true to Chaucer's method of composition—punctuation of any kind rarely is—for it instructs the reader to make a connection where Chaucer has successfully failed to do so. His *modus operandi* seems better described by my earlier image, that of a marriage: the bed is not a single one occupied only by a candidly sweet damsel (line one), but a double one shared by a not altogether congruent gentleman (line two). They are evidently some species of spouse, but each possesses its own syntactical integrity, each is a grammatical entity that can and does exist without its companion, yet it exists also in some sort of relationship with its companion. To define the nature of this relationship, however, is not something Chaucer has troubled to do. Like Pandarus, he has tossed the gentleman into bed with the lady and withdrawn to the fireplace. They must figure out their own relationship, which means that we must. And unlike Pandarus, Chaucer will provide no further assistance.

The relationship must be inferred by the reader, and no two readers will make precisely the same inference. Much will depend upon one's moral and intellectual predispositions. Nowadays, when Chaucer is often presented as a better teacher than Aquinas (though not quite up to Augustine), many will fill the syntactical void with a moralization, a procedure which generally results in the total obliteration of Spouse A by Spouse B. Now I acknowledge that with the second couplet I have quoted moralization is probably the only solution: line two, asserting the Friar's expertise at begging, if it does not wholly negate line one, asserting his virtue, certainly forces a radical redefinition of it. When we come upon the phrase 'a virtuous man', our instinct—and that of Chaucer's first readers—is to take the phrase in its broadest sense, to give a fellow human being the benefit of the doubt, even though at this point in the Friar's portrait we will find it hard to do so. But of course line two makes us redefine the *vertuous* of line one as 'efficacious', and little remains of line one's clear statement except the memory of the ideal of that virtuous man which everything in the Friar's life has perverted.

Yet moralization is by no means the inevitable solution when we are faced by the voids created by Chaucer's lucid clarity. For what of the Wife of Bath? The relationship between the Wife of Bath's being a worthy woman all her life and having had five husbands is a long way from unequivocal. Of course it isn't if one assumes that Chaucer agreed with St. Paul, St. Jerome, and other male saints on the subject of women and wives; to such people five husbands are clearly *de trop*, and those who don't like the Wife will consider her wicked and doomed, while those who do like her, or would like to, will consider her somehow tragic (and doomed). For the moralist, line two must cancel line one or at least force him to make a radical redefinition of the word *worthy*. But the trouble is that we have no lexicographical authority to do so: *worthy* seems to mean 'worthy'. Therefore it is my feeling that Chaucer called the Wife of Bath a worthy woman because he thought she *was* a worthy woman, either despite or on account of five husbands. Indeed, the two lines are an epitome of the Wife of Bath, portrait, prologue, and tale: they encapsulate the problem she presents. It is true that the aforementioned holy men had what they considered an easy solution, which was to suppress the problem by suppressing Wives of Bath and indeed all women non-saints; and it is fashionable to assert that Chaucer agreed with their solution through cultural necessity. But these lines present no evidence that he did: the Wife was a worthy woman all her life, and she comes out of Chaucer's fiction with more life in her than many of us nonfictions possess. Indeed, I should not be surprised if the correct way of reading the couplet is to adopt its mathematical suggestion—that one perdurably vital woman has more worthiness, is worth more, than any five random males at church door. I said 'correct', but that is of course the wrong word, for there can be no right answer. While we may feel that we have been invited to answer a question, the fact is that none has actually been asked. We have to read between the lines in order to find the question itself, and naturally the question we find is the one to which we have thought up an answer. And all this inconclusive work we have done in response to Chaucer's simple straightforward statements.

I have been dealing with small examples of Chaucer's creation of the problematical through the appearance of clarity. I should like now to move on to more substantial ones in his *Troilus and Criseide*—indeed, ones which are of large importance to the way we end up thinking about the two persons of the title. Let me start by considering the matter of Criseide's social situation in Troy as it appears at the beginning of the poem. She is first introduced after a four-stanza account of Calchas' treachery, which concludes with the frightening reaction to his misbehaviour of the Trojan populace, who say that

> . . . he and al his kin atones
> Been worthy for to brennen, fel and bones. (I, 90–1)

Then we come to the threatened heroine:

> Now hadde Calcas lefte in this mischaunce,
> Al unwist of this false and wikked deede,
> His doughter, which that was in greet penaunce,
> For of hir lif she was ful sore in drede,
> As she that niste what was best to rede;
> For bothe a widwe was she, and allone
> Of any freend to whom she dorste mone. (92–8)

'For she was both a widow and alone of any friend'. Since the expression 'alone of' does not occur in Modern English, I am uncertain how to translate it: should one say merely 'without', or else 'alone without'? Actually, it doesn't matter: regardless of which the phrase properly means in Modern English, Chaucer's Middle English has succeeded in getting in the notion of loneliness, aloneness. Indeed, as the line fades from memory, the sense it leaves is that Criseide was friendless *and* alone. And this is of course precisely what Chaucer wished to achieve: it is the sense of Criseide's being alone that he emphasizes both in her visit to request Hector's protection (106–26) and in her appearance in the temple at the Feast of the Palladion, where Troilus first sees her standing 'ful lowe and stille, allone' (178). Since she is very beautiful, this loneliness seems a violation of nature and makes her all the more poignantly the object of our sympathy—a damsel in distress if there ever was one.

This impression is only partly dissipated by a stanza that Chaucer gives us concerning her life in Troy after Hector has promised his protection:

> And in hir hous she abood with swich meinee
> As til hir honour neede was to holde,
> And whil she was dwelling in that citee
> Kepte hir estaat, and bothe of yonge and olde
> Ful wel biloved, and wel men of hire tolde. (127–31)

She had a house (not at this time called a palace) and a *meinee*, a household, sufficient to her honour, and people spoke well of her. Any reader who had got the impression (as he almost might have) that she lived alone in a one-room walk-up in an unfashionable part of town would be disabused. But I don't think he would be quite prepared for the facts of the case as they are presented at the beginning of Book II, when Pandarus seizes the occasion of a bright May morning to visit her on Troilus' behalf:

> When he was come into his neces place,
> 'Where is my lady?' to hir folk quod he.
> And they him tolde, and he forth in gan pace,
> And foond two othere ladies sete and she
> Within a paved parlour, and they three
> Herden a maiden reden hem the geste
> Of the sege of Thebes whil hem leste.
>
> Quod Pandarus, 'Madame, God you see,
> With al youre book and al the compaignye.'
> 'Ey, uncle myn, welcome, ywis,' quod she.
> And up she roos, and by the hand in hie
> She took him faste, and saide, 'This night thrie—
> To goode mote it turne—of you I mette.'
> And with that word she down on benche him sette.
>
> 'Ye, nece, ye shal faren wel the bet,
> If God wol, al this yeer,' quod Pandarus. (II, 78–93)

Now an inventory of Criseide's social situation would include the following: Item, folk, an unknown number but still enough to be called folk, who were her servants and met Pandarus at the door; Item, two other ladies in the paved parlour besides 'she'—Chaucer seems so tender towards Criseide that he won't even put her in the objective case (though actually she'd been in the objective since Western Europe forgot Greek); Item, one book with one literate maiden reading it aloud; and, finally and most important, one uncle, well enough known to be admitted without announcement, on easy enough terms with Criseide so that they fall at once—with Criseide leading—into affectionate, rather flirtatious banter about dreams—apparently old and good friends. One can only conclude that Chaucer's original statement about Criseide's being 'alone of any friend' was misleading, to say the least. Whoever her husband was, he had left her well off, and that *meinee* she kept was a large one: later, three of the ladies who formed part of her household are given names (II, 816), and include at least two nieces, while the total number of women-in-waiting is said to form 'a greet route' (II, 818)—a large crowd. And then, of course, there was uncle Pandarus, always ready with advice and news, a man eminent enough in Troy so that (as we learn later) he sometimes has to spend the whole day with King Priam (V, 281–5), and is the best friend of Hector's young brother Troilus.

Yet the powerful impression of a woman in danger, alone, which is the first impression we have of Criseide, while it may not and does not entirely square with the facts as the narrative develops, is an enormously important one and one which is never entirely cancelled out. On the one hand she is a kind of archetypal romance heroine, the lovely lady distressed, engaging our sympathy both because she is beautiful and because she is helpless, in need of a romance hero to succour her and keep her safe. It is this aspect of her upon which Pandarus plays so skilfully and so cruelly when he invents a legal harassment by such worthies as Aeneas (II, 1464–77). On the other hand, romance heroines do not ever really exist, while Criseide does: within a Troy that is not only the fabled city of literary antiquity but also fourteenth-century London, Criseide has another mode of being—an intelligent, perceptive, self-assured, well-to-do woman who knows her way around in society and who even comes close to knowing her own mind. But the paradox of Criseide is that she really is both these very different people—which is why accounts of her in criticism are so wildly divergent: some scholars see her as the helpless pawn of cruel Fortune, others as a woman who sensibly adjusts to the inevitable. And as a matter of fact, they are all correct, depending upon what elements in her are chosen for emphasis. C. S. Lewis found the key to her in the line which calls her 'the ferfulleste wight that mighte be' (II, 450-1); Karl Young used to pursue those lines in which the poet tells us 'she was wis' (III, 86) with a dark suspicion that allowed little merit to a woman's possessing intelligence; and once after I had given what I thought was a very tender account of Criseide's infidelity, an eminent lady scholar told me angrily that I should be ashamed of myself for slandering that lovely girl. It is evident that Criseide is many things to many people.

And that is Chaucer's fault—and I suppose his intention—for what he tells us about her is contradictory, so that we have an option about what to believe. Indeed, he not only gives us an option, he encourages us to write our own story by giving us insufficient information, and doing so aggressively. The last couplet of a stanza I quoted a while ago is an example:

> But wheither that she children hadde or noon,
> I rede it nought, therefore I late it goon. (I,132-3)

While there have been articles published on the Wife of Bath's children, or lack of them, so far as I know no one has speculated about Criseide's progeny: I guess everyone is satisfied that her husband died without issue. That is because on the whole readers tend to agree that a romance heroine has no business being initially encumbered with nurslings. Yet by bringing up this issue and leaving it unsettled Chaucer has, of course, reminded us that his romance heroine has non-romance potentialities. And the matter of children may bring up in some minds the matter of Criseide's late husband, who doesn't even have a name. One could get along very well without the name if one had some inkling about their marital relationship. Romance convention generally prefers that its heroines be *tabulae rasae*, emotionally speaking, and I like to think that Criseide's husband was like one of the Wife of Bath's first three, an elderly man of means who paid little attention to her, and whose death, despite her rather ostentatious mourning, she never really much lamented. This enables her—for me—to retain the essentials of her romance role. But if she was happily married, then one's basic assumptions about her are altered—and we do have her word that she at least loved her husband:

'But as to speke of love, ywis,' she saide,
'I hadde a lord to whom I wedded was,
The whos myn herte al was til that he deide.' (V, 974–6)

But she is speaking here to Diomede, and if what she has just said is not a lie (as we hope it is), what follows it is surely mendacious:

And other love, as helpe me now Pallas,
Ther in myn herte nis ne nevere was. (977–8)

Nevertheless, to some readers the dead husband will always remain a disconcerting factor in their estimate of Criseide—they will feel as if they had come to a play late, missing the premises upon which the action is based; and, since Criseide does betray the role of romance heroine, they will be forced to readjust their image of her, and do so by filling in her earlier life in a way which would better explain her later action. Chaucer loves this kind of manipulation of the reader, and actually concludes his last description of Criseide—that wonderfully sad passage that occurs so surprisingly midway through Book V—with the fiendishly mischievous line:

But trewely, I can nat telle hir age. (826)

One has a horrible moment of supposing that her age all along might have been highly relevant to her behaviour. But in fact one realizes that Criseide's age is just another unknown in a world that consists mostly of unknowns.

If Criseide is at least sporadically a romance heroine, her opposite number scarcely qualifies as a romance hero at all. It is frequently said that Troilus is a typical courtly lover, but this can be true only in the sense that he could figure as the speaker of a brief Provençal lyric of unrequited love. But it is evident that when he is transferred into a high romance he has got himself into the wrong genre. Paralysis is all very well for under a hundred complaining lines, but more than eight thousand lines of a hero's inaction do not leave us with much impression of heroism. I do not wish to appear scornful of Troilus: he is a far better man than, say, Lancelot, and almost all his qualities are admirable. But while Chaucer and others within the poem keep assuring us that on the battlefield Troilus was a terror, the poet, having resolved not to sing of the arms of the man, never shows us Troilus actively at work in war. And in the bedroom, which is where we generally see him, he seems entirely too intellectual, too unconfident, too introspective to give any impression of heroism. He has, as Criseide perceives (IV, 1672), moral virtue grounded upon troth, and he is wholly admirable as a citizen of Troy or anywhere else. But the poet makes little attempt to adapt his character to the requirements of high romance, beyond, of course, allowing him to love Criseide with a high passion, and even this passion is over-disciplined. Yet at one very important point in the poem Chaucer does make an effort, albeit an abortive one, to render Troilus heroic; this is at the point where the necessity to be a romance hero conflicts most squarely with the necessity to be a good citizen— the problem of what to do about Criseide's exchange for Antenor.

Once the exchange has been arranged and ratified by Priam and parliament, the most obvious recourse for the romantic hero that Troilus ought to be is to take Pandarus' suggestion (which Troilus himself had thought of (IV, 530, 542)) and forcibly prevent Criseide's departure by kidnapping her. Pandarus and Troilus discuss this plan several times, and Pandarus is willing to die while executing it (IV, 624–8). But Troilus will not consent to it unless Criseide herself consents to it. Yet the strange truth is that the plan is never proposed to Criseide at all. Before his last night with her Troilus assures Pandarus that he will discuss the proposal with her, though at the same time he notes that Troy is in its present predicament because of the kidnapping of a woman, and that for him to violate an approved treaty would be treasonable (IV, 547–60). Whether it is this that weighs upon him when he is with Criseide, or whether it is because he instinctively knows that she would not sanction her own kidnapping, Chaucer does not say. But rather than suggest this course of action to her, Troilus suggests a modified version: that they should steal away together (IV, 1503). Of an idea so shamefully unheroic Criseide is rightly scornful—indeed, the repetition of the proposal by Troilus near the end of the scene is his lowest point as a hero (IV, 1601). One feels that he is being more womanly than she, and I am sure many readers momentarily feel, with Diomede, that he is a fool who will forget himself (V, 98). In any case, the plan to kidnap Criseide is never mentioned to her; it is not within Troilus' power even to propose it, much less to execute it.

But it is not forgotten by Chaucer, for the next morning when Diomede is waiting to escort Criseide to the Greek camp, and Troilus comes to make his farewell and watch her departure, the plan reappears. Troilus rides near,

> So wo-bigoon, al wolde he nought him plaine,
> That on his hors unnethe he sat for paine.
>
> For ire he quook, so gan his herte gnawe
> Whan Diomede on hors gan him to dresse,
> And saide to himself this ilke sawe,
> 'Allas,' quod he, 'thus foul a wrecchednesse,
> Why suffre ich it? Why nil ich it redresse?
> Were it nat bet atones for to die
> Than everemore in langour thus to crye?
>
> Why nil I make at ones riche and poore
> To have ynough to doon er that she go?
> Why nil I bringe al Troye upon a rore?
> Why nil I sleen this Diomede also?
> Why nil I rather with a man or two
> Stele hire away? Why wol I this endure?
> Why nil I helpen to myn owne cure?' (V, 34-49)

Rhetorical questions generally need no answers and certainly these do not. We know very well why Troilus will not help to his own cure—we've heard at length through the previous book how his ideals prevent him. Nevertheless we know what Lancelot would have done, what he so often did do, rescuing Guinevere with ruthless force; and what Gawain would have done; what even a second-class romance hero would have attempted, and we can't help letting some feeling of disappointment mingle with our admiration for Troilus. And the narrator, anticipating our disappointment and as it were guiltily aware that he and Troilus are letting the romance public down, leaps in with a chivalric reason for his hero's inaction:

> But why he nolde doon so fel a deede
> That shal I sayn, and why him liste it spare:
> He hadde in herte alwayes a manere drede
> Lest that Criseide, in rumour of this fare,
> Sholde han been slain—lo, this was al his care,
> And elles certain, as I saide yore,
> He hadde it doon withouten wordes more. (50–6)

It is interesting that in this case not even Troilus knew the reasons that the narrator knew he knew. And while the motives for abstention that are given are, as I said, chivalric, they are rather timidly chivalric. One of Chaucer's rare attempts to turn his hero into a proper romance hero is thwarted by his hero's nature: he can't even invent a satisfactory lie about him.

Yet if Criseide is only sporadically a romance heroine and Troilus almost not a romance hero at all, the fact is that they are engaged in a real romance, and that the poem itself can only be described as a great romance. And involvement in romance does succeed in redefining us all, if only momentarily and illusorily. Hence it is interesting to observe what Chaucer does at the culminating moment of the romance—the consummation scene in Book III—to see to it that his hero and heroine rise to the occasion.

You will recall the circumstances. Criseide and a number of her women have come to dinner at Pandarus' palace, where the carefully foreseen rainstorm forces them to spend the night. Criseide is placed in a room that is accessible only through two other rooms —according to Pandarus—in the middle one of which Criseide's women are lodged and in the outer one Pandarus himself. But then there is the trap-door into Criseide's room, through which, after infinite delay while he argues with Criseide, Pandarus finally leads Troilus (I note that in genuinely heroic romance fashion poor Troilus has been hidden in a closet in the house since midnight the night before—a sojourn of some twenty hours (III, 599–602).) Once Troilus is introduced to the bedroom he finds that Pandarus has cast him in the role of a jealous lover and that Criseide is—or seems to his extraordinary sensitivity—angry with him. Whereupon he faints, disqualifying himself entirely from any international competition for lovers in romance. But the fainting enables Pandarus to strip him down to the bare shirt and cast him into bed, where he and Criseide give him such treatment as they can to revive him. As for Criseide

> . . . to deliveren him fro bittre bondes
> She ofte him kiste. And shortly for to sayne,
> Him to revoken she dide al hir paine. (III, 1116–18)

Finally—and with what devilishness Chaucer prolongs the faint just one stanza beyond the reader's expectation—Troilus begins to revive, and asks:

> . . . O mercy God, what thing is this? (1124)

Criseide responds with her own question:

> 'Why do ye with youreselven thus amis?'
> Quod tho Criseide. 'Is this a mannes game?
> What, Troilus, wol ye do thus for shame?' (1125–7)

But the rebuke is only verbal:

> And therwithal hir arm over him she laide,
> And al foryaf, and ofte time him keste. (1128–9)

At this moment Pandarus, who some time earlier had retired to the fire, where he

> ... took a light, and foond his countenaunce
> As for to looke upon an old romaunce, (979–80)

but whose contemplation of romance Troilus' fainting had interrupted, retires again:

> Quod Pandarus, 'For ought I can espyen,
> This light nor I ne serven here of nought.
> Light is nought good for sike folkes yën.
> But for the love of God, sin ye been brought
> In thus good plit, lat now no hevy thought
> Been hanging in the hertes of you tweye'—
> And bar the candel to the chimineye. (1135–41)

Criseide has kissed Troilus oft-times—actually twice oft-times—and has forgiven him, while Pandarus has retired to the indefinitely located fire-place. One might suppose that Troilus would see his way clear to behaving like a lover; the poet comments that Criseide saw no cause to ask him to leave (1144–5). But no, Troilus allows himself to be drawn into a six-stanza rediscussion of the jealousy matter. At the end of this passage, Criseide forgives him —for the third time, though the first time he had been unconscious—and then she reverses the role of grantor and suppliant:

> 'And now,' quod she, 'that I have doon you smerte,
> Foryive it me, myn owne sweete herte.' (1182–3)

This graciousness finally brings Troilus into action:

> This Troilus, with blisse of that supprised,
> Putte al in Goddes hand, as he that mente
> Nothing but wel, and sodeinly avised,
> He hire in armes faste to him hente;
> And Pandarus, with a ful good entente,
> Laide him to sleepe and saide, 'If ye be wise,
> Swouneth nought now, lest more folk arise.' (1184–90)

This is one of the most delightful stanzas in Chaucer's works. Troilus, in being surprised by the bliss of *that*—the pronoun presumably refers to Criseide's asking for forgiveness—would be, I imagine, unique among romance heroes, no other one of whom would be surprised at this point in the affair; and for him to put all in God's hand (meaning nothing but well) is also uniquely Troilian: surely the notion that the hero is taking some great risk here would be shared by few lovers and is shared by few readers. And to his being 'suddenly advised', one can only sigh, 'Well, it's about time', which is what Chaucer allows Pandarus, from his topological no man's land, to do for us. You might, indeed, say that the consummation of a love affair never got off to a worse start, with a hero timid to the point of recalcitrance, a heroine who has had to administer first-aid to her swooning lover, and a far from innocent bystander making apropos but uncalled-for editorial comments.

Fortunately, however, Chaucer's narrator doesn't know that there is anything unusual about the scene, which he seems to take for granted. But while literary precedents dealing with preliminaries seem to have eluded him, he has read a number of old books which tell of consummations, and he knows the literary rules for such events, and is determined to apply them: heroines of course are fragile little creatures embraced by fiercely impetuous military gentlemen—or larks in the clutches of sparrow-hawks:

> What mighte or may the sely larke saye
> Whan that the sperhawk hath him in his foot?
> I can namore, but of thise ilke twaye,
> To whom this tale sucre be or soot.
> Though that I tarye a yeer, som time I moot
> After myn auctour tellen hir gladnesse,
> As wel as I have told hir hevinesse.

> Criseide, which that felte hire thus ytake—
> As writen clerkes in hir bookes olde—
> Right as an aspes leef she gan to quake,
> Whan she him felte hire in his armes folde. (1191–201)

Chaucer is an honest scholar. Readers could find reason—as I fear I have been doing—to doubt whether Criseide at this point would

D

be actually quaking like an aspen leaf; and so Chaucer documents the statement with a footnote, which he places right in the middle of the text:

> As writen clerkes in hir bookes olde.

And of course he's right: that's what clerks say heroines do in these circumstances, and what Chaucer's author said Criseide did —even though it may take Chaucer a year to get around to telling us about it.

But the fact is that the roles I have been examining are, by Chaucer's transparent sleight-of-hand, changing, and the timid Troilus is actually becoming the confident romance hero, while the knowledgeable Criseide somehow does fulfil the part of the timid heroine of songs and stories old. The final step in the transition is the famous exchange between the two that occurs just after the stanza last quoted:

> This Troilus in armes gan hire straine,
> And saide, 'O sweete, as evere mote I goon,
> Now be ye caught, now is ther but we twaine.
> Now yeeldeth you, for other boote is noon.'
> To that Criseide answerde thus anoon,
> 'Nadde I er now, my sweete herte dere,
> Been yolde, ywis, I were now nought here.' (1205–11)

Troilus now sees himself in his proper role, an aggressive male who has, after long pursuit, caught the lady, and she must perforce give in: 'Now yeeldeth you.' Criseide's reply mediates precisely between her real role and her romance one: on the one hand she is acknowledging the truth of the charges that scholars are always making (and that I have been making) that she always knew well enough what she was doing and what she wanted to have happen; on the other hand, her yielding is infinitely romantic, charming above any heroine's yielding that I have encountered in poetry, and even more flattering to the lover's sense of his worth because of the suggestion of her forethought and

connivance. Criseide's reply is a kind of touchstone for deter-
mining critical attitudes towards her, for every critic betrays his
bias in what he says about this passage: to some it proves that she
was a true daughter of Calchas, calculating; to others, it
displays a generosity enhanced by wit that is rare in the best of
heroines, a triumphantly romantic surrender to love. Neither
opinion is true, because both are.

I fear I have been overcrowding the bedroom in Pandarus'
house, which is crowded enough as it is, what with Criseide,
Troilus, Pandarus, Chaucer, an old author or two, and the reader.
To increase the number by multiplying Criseide and Troilus each
into two different persons brings the cast up to ghetto conditions.
Happily in the remainder of the scene Chaucer provides a less
crowded stage. With the disappearance (or silence) of Pandarus,
the intrusion of one order of reality ceases, and with its cessation
the two lovers, in relative privacy, devote themselves to the roles
that romance demands of them. And they do so with high passion,
having been, finally, redefined by romance:

> Criseide, al quit from every drede and teene,
> As she that juste cause hadde him to triste,
> Made him swich feeste it joye was to seene,
> Whan she his trouthe and clene entente wiste:
> And as aboute a tree, with many a twiste,
> Bitrent and writh the sweete wodebinde,
> Gan eech of hem in armes other winde. (1226–32)

I doubt that many readers will care to wonder what it is that has
suddenly freed Criseide from dreads and vexations, what has suddenly given her just cause to trust Troilus, why it is only now that
she recognizes his troth and clean intent. Caught up on the wings
of poetry, we accept unhesitatingly that everything the poet says is
true, for the intensity of the emotion is far more powerful than
adherence to a truth that has, at least for the moment, become
merely petty. A few stanzas back we might have smiled, as I think
we should have, when Criseide became a *sely larke*, a poor innocent bird caught in the claws of a hawk. But I think that few will
smile at her becoming a nightingale:

And as the newe abaised nightingale,
That stinteth first whan she biginneth singe,
Whan that she heereth any hierde tale,
Or in the hegges any wight stiringe,
And after siker dooth hir vois out ringe,
Right so Criseide, whan she hir drede stente,
Opened hir herte and tolde him hir entente. (1233–9)

This may not be the way things really would have happened between the Criseide and Troilus we think we have come to know. But if it is not expected realism, it is something a good deal better—an illusion, perhaps, but one that makes the potentialities of reality come truer than fact itself, an illusion that no reader of romance would trade for all the facts in the world. Chaucer, having given us not very likely characters for his love story, has transformed them to meet the demands of romance. That the metamorphosis effected by love is, from history's point of view, as transitory as it is illusory is the sad subject of the rest of the poem. But it is a bold and boldly misguided reader who would cancel out for whatever reasons, moral or historical, the marvellous illusion that Chaucer creates for us in the remainder of the third book of *Troilus*.

Who knows if all that Chaucer wrote was true?

asks Henryson of *Troilus and Criseide*. I should not know how to reply; it is, or it isn't, or it ought to have been. For Chaucer truth was never simple, always so qualified that the only way to express it satisfactorily was to mix statements of fact with many contradictory truths. In a way, the image of his poetry is that of the false report and the true one which unite inseparably to get out of the House of Rumor into history. To try to analyse the 'truth' in poetry of this kind is at best humiliating, and one can only confess that, compared with the poetry, the best in this critical kind are but shadows, and neither learning nor imagination much amends them.

I should like to conclude by glancing at a passage that seems to me the epitome of the Chaucerian love of diaphanously clear statements utterly destructive of one another's meaning. This comes at the end of the Nun's Priest's well-known if inconclusive discussion of free will and necessity. Having outlined the theories of Augustine, Boethius, and Bradwardine, he breaks off in something like despair:

> I wol nat han to do of swich matere:
> My tale is of a cok, as ye may heere,
> That took his conseil of his wif with sorwe,
> To walken in the yeerd upon that morwe
> That he hadde met the dreem that I you tolde.
> Wommenes conseils been ful ofte colde,
> Wommanes conseil broughte us first to wo,
> And made Adam fro Paradis to go,
> Theras he was ful merye and wel at ease.
> But for I noot to whom it mighte displese
> If I conseil of wommen sholde blame,
> Passe over, for I saide it in my game—
> Rede auctours wher they trete of swich matere,
> And what they sayn of wommen ye may heere—
> Thise been the cokkes wordes and nat mine:
> I can noon harm of no womman divine. (CT, B 4441–56)

I have exhausted my ration of butterflies to be broken on the wheel of criticism for one day at least, and even if I hadn't, I should be reluctant to tackle this series of truths, half-truths, and contradictory truths, this series of aggressions and elusions.

> I wol nat han to do of swich matere.

Nevertheless, I cannot help observing that the cast of speakers of this soliloquy is almost as large as the cast of characters in the bedroom in Pandarus' house, for it includes Chaucer, the Nun's Priest, Chauntecleer, Pertelote, the reader (male), the reader (female), Adam, the Prioress, old authors, and heaven knows who else. All of them seem to be having their say in some corner of a line, and what each says is true and valid, even if it denies what someone else is saying simultaneously. Everything is clear and clearly right. And if the Nun's Priest has not already solved the problem of women—as far as any man is likely to solve it—with his (or Chauntecleer's) translation,

> *Mulier est hominis confusio:*
> Madame, the sentence of this Latin is,
> 'Womman is mannes joye and al his blis,' (B 4354–6)

he tries again here:

> Wommenes conseils been ful ofte colde;

still,

> I can noon harm of no woman divine.

And if any woman, including the charming and learned scholar to whom this volume is dedicated, feels that these paradoxes are those of a male chauvinist swine, I remind her that

> These been the Nun's Priest's wordës, and nat mine.

IV

An Argumentative Muse:
A Background for the 'University Wits'

S. GORLEY PUTT

WHEN the 'University Wits'—Marlowe, Lyly, Peele, Kyd, Greene, and the rest of them—found employment in the new theatre industry of London in the 1580's, their activities were as fresh, and as predictable, as those of the playwrights of our own day who have found in the radio and television industry a similar challenge. In each case they found a new audience and a new medium; in each case they could not forget, even if they wished to do so, habits of dramatic presentation inherited from pre-Henslowe and pre-B.B.C. days. To the literary historian, it is the freshness that makes the more vivid impression. A play like George Peele's *The Arraignment of Paris* (1584) is chock-full of instances of the way in which these young 'University Wits' took advantage of the various aids to entertainment supplied by new techniques—in this particular case interpreted by a cast of youthful scholars and choristers. In some of its verse passages it strikes notes which re-echo in Shakespeare and later dramatists. Most interestingly of all, it exhibits—with a fine catholicity of taste becoming to an enterprising scholar still in his twenties— various other ways, literary and thematic, in which the new theatrical productions might just as well have developed. It is an unashamedly courtly pastoral, light and yet touching at times on personal and political truths. It assumes in its audience both an easy familiarity with classical mythology and also a witty recognition of the way in which this polite new learning could be pillaged for *doubles entendres* and topical references. It is gay, deft, mocking and serious. It abounds in songs and dances for the delight of a music-loving metropolitan *élite*. It must have made, for after-dinner courtly listeners, an enchanting cabaret.

Yet the indebtedness of these scholarly youngsters to their fore-bears has also been thoroughly investigated. The very notion of 'Renaissance' has either been denied, pushed backwards in time to embrace much that previously passed as 'medieval', or at least found to embody and perpetuate much of the medieval pattern of thought; and in this general revaluation the Elizabethan theatre has not been overlooked. In the following notes I wish to review briefly the bearing on the experiments in entertainment practised by these young Elizabethan graduates of two well-established earlier conventions: the persistent intellectual assumptions of 'courtly love', argued and systematized for several centuries, and the more recent habits of abstract argumentation as presented dramatically in the Tudor court interludes.

Justifiably puzzled by the hold over men's imagination exercised for so long a time by the strange Provençal convention of 'courtly love', which has stirred the comments of scores of literary historians without ever producing a really convincing explanation, of its origin and attraction, a recent American critic has this to say:

What it all meant will perhaps remain for ever a riddle. It has been represented as a heresy, a social game, a nervous revolt against Christian ascetical precepts, an allegory. . . . To aristo-crats it seems indeed to have been a game, largely conversational, which may have produced sometimes a real live assignation or affair.[1]

'Andreas the Chaplain's' guide to the rules and regulations governing courtly love as practised at the end of the twelfth century[2] may be selected as one introduction to that strange social convention of medieval provincial courts, which is reflected in

---

[1] Donald R. Howard, 'Literature and Sexuality', *The Massachusetts Review*, VIII, 3 (1967).
[2] Andreas Capellanus, *The Art of Courtly Love*, tr. and ed. J. J. Parry (N.Y., 1941).

Chrétien de Troyes, Boccaccio, and Chaucer, and later in Renaissance versions rehashed in such Italianate romances as *A Petite Pallace of Pettie His Pleasure*, providing plots and some lingering traces of style for Shakespeare and his fellow-dramatists. (Even in the eighteenth century there are echoes, in Sterne and the sentimental novel; and some of the platitudes, aphorisms, quibbles, and entrenched legends about lovers—their paleness, sleeplessness, and lack of appetite—are widely repeated even today.) In *The Art of Courtly Love* there are jumbled together scraps of allegory and dream-stories, and some pearls of sage nonsense: 'The man who thinks he can please a wise woman by doing something foolish shows a great lack of sense.' The habits of medieval education are apparent throughout in the debating technique with innumerable references to 'authorities', classical and biblical. Solomon and Cato are impartially called upon to support the most obvious remarks. The longevity of this system of placing down all possible attitudes to a problem and selecting no final solution is as remarkable as that of the subject matter; Milton's *L'Allegro* and *Il Penseroso* are the result of an almost unchanged training in disquisition. The good chaplain sees fit to cancel all his tortuous instructions about nicely-graded etiquette and how to speak pretty amorous syllogisms in a final chapter on 'The Rejection of Love'. This is about as convincing as Chaucer's pious renunciations, and one would as soon father Proust as Andreas with the statement: 'There is nothing in the world more loathsome or more wearisome than to meditate too intently on the nature or the characteristics of a woman.'

The young Elizabethan University Wit who brought into the theatre something of the content and manner of this seemingly indestructible tradition was John Lyly. He first added his contribution to this long and mysteriously attractive medieval heritage by a prose romance, *Euphues, the Anatomy of Wit* (1579), which won instant popularity in court circles and has added a name to English literary history—'euphuism'—as a description of the kind of writing it helped to make fashionable. When applied to drama, Lyly's achievement was remarkable enough to deserve the high claim made on his behalf by Professor Wilson Knight: 'The stream of romantic love welling from Provence and fertilizing medieval allegory is locked now in the tight reservoirs of Lyly's dramatic work, forming new depths.'[1] But although Lyly's grace and allusive balance have rightly earned him a trade-mark monopoly for this kind of writing in English, it is useful to remember that many similar experiments, some earlier than his own, were being made by exuberant Elizabethan tellers of romantic tales— tales which the over-worked suppliers of material for the new theatres, hack-writers and genuine poets alike, pillaged without shame.

One of their most popular quarries was the curious compilation of continental-style romances printed three years before *Euphues*— *A Petite Pallace of Pettie His Pleasure*.[2] The most surprising thing about George Pettie's *Pallace* is that it may still be read with pleasure. Recent revivals of what may be termed the old rag-bag type of novel, stuffed with a miscellaneous load of observations and impressions, can reconcile a modern reader to 'the strenuous designs of latticed prose' (in the words of Pettie's editor, H. W. Hartman) of the earliest English novels. For all its elaborate variations on well-worn saws (well-worn in the sixteenth century and almost threadbare today), there remains in the *Pallace* a sufficient number of pertinent comments to make the work readable by those who, like the 'gentle Gentlewomen' who first turned its pages, approach it with more than an eye for style alone.

Not that Pettie and his like, including Lyly, can claim merit as pure narrators. He is content to borrow his plots from Ovid, Livy, Hyginus, Castiglione, and many others, and he is woefully unaware of the first principles of selection or emphasis. Yet the laboured accuracy of the following passage, to take only one example, although reading almost like a parody of Proust, certainly displays more than a passing interest in human behaviour:

---

[1] G. Wilson Knight: 'Lyly', in *Elizabethan Drama: Modern Essays in Criticism* (ed. R. J. Kaufmann (N.Y., 1961); reprinted from *Review of English Studies*, XV, April 1939).

[2] *A Petite Pallace of Pettie His Pleasure*, ed. Herbert W. Hartman (1938).

For as the finest meates that bee, eaten by one in extremity of
sicknesse, resolve not to pure bloud to strengthen the body, but
to watrish humors to feede the fever and disease: so though her
face and lookes were fine and sweete, and brought delight to all
the beholders els, yet to him they wrought onely torment and
trouble of minde: and notwithstanding hee perceived her beauty
to breed his bane, & her lookes to procure the losse of his
liberty . . . yet could he not refrain his eyes from beholding her,
but according to the nature of the sickly pacient, which cheifly
desireth that which cheiflye is forbidden him, hee so incessently
threw his amarous glaunces towards her. . . .

And in spite of the prophetic 'euphuism' of the style, there is in
Pettie's occasional use of good idiomatic speech a certain liveliness
of movement more characteristic of his playwright successors:

in came *Itys* the prety elfe beeing two or three yeeres of age, and
seeing his mother sit sadly sayd unto her, Mam how doost, why
doest weepe, and tooke her about the necke and kist her, saying,
I will goe and call my dad to come and play with thee . . . the
infant rose againe, and came run dugling to her saying, why do
you beate me mam, I have learned my Criscrosse today so I
have, and my father sayth hee wil buie mee a golden coate, and
then you shannot kisse mee so you shannot . . .

'At a time when proverbial wisdom was in the air,' writes
Professor Hartman, 'sitters in the sun bettered their grandsires'
maxims and beldames quoted Seneca unwittingly.' Pettie's thiev-
ing of 'sentences' is shameless, simply because to the writer or
adapter of *novelle* no shame could be attributed to such deliberate
anthologizing. Just as a young law student, a century and a half
later, read the pastorals of Fontenelle 'with a design to collect some
little hints for conversation with the ladies',[1] so Pettie's public
would read and re-read the elegant passages between hesitant
lovers, and copy down gems from the abundant correspondence.
Pettie's *exempla* were lifted from many varied sources (it is interesting to note how many came direct from Heywood's *Dialogue*

[1] *The Diary of Dudley Ryder 1715–1716*, ed. W. Matthews (1939).

conteynyng the number of the effectuall prouerbes in the Englische tounge, 1546) of what his editor happily terms this 'ubiquitous pollen of humanism'. His extravagances of patterned speech ('O heavens why heape you my heavinesse? O planets why plant you my paine?'), no less than his more acceptable alliterative vigour ('lastly in olde age wee covetously carke for coine, wee toyle for trashe'), uphold Pettie's claim to stand beside Lyly as at least the godfather of 'euphuism'.

However much literary historians may vary in the degree of scepticism with which they view the so-called 'convention of courtly love' (and members of the English Association who heard Professor Talbot Donaldson's recent lecture will know that at least one expert is profoundly sceptical),[1] there is no doubt that both in its early forms and in its later Anglicized adulterations it helped to keep alive for a remarkably long period a literary habit of psychological argumentation. I notice that twice already I have invoked, without design, the name of Marcel Proust. I am reminded that, although our own century has spawned a wonderful new vocabulary for the discussion of psychological and sociological problems, it would be very naïve to suppose that we were the first people solemnly to debate these matters. By the time the University Wits arrived upon the scene, at any rate, English readers of romances and English courtiers attending the performance of Tudor interludes had been invited to engage in abstract psychological and sociological speculations so wide in range and so varied in depth that they could be linked, on the one hand with the musings of some remote cogitative Montaigne, and on the other hand with the dogged argumentative persistence of a Launcelot Gobbo.

It is a commonplace of literary history that the Tudor court interlude developed from the secularization of the morality play. Indeed, many dramatic habits based on the moralities lasted well beyond the time of the University Wits, if we are to believe the plausible thesis of a modern scholar who has tracked down

---

[1] E. Talbot Donaldson, 'Chaucer and the Elusion of Clarity', a lecture delivered to The English Association on 16 October 1971, and reprinted in the present volume.

examples of the conditioned reflexes of moralities and moral interludes in works by Greene and Lodge, Marston, Dekker, Middleton, Ben Jonson, and Thomas Heywood.[1] It should be noted in passing that the real change of emphasis lies in the extension of the area of argument: the church-based moralities themselves naturally had only one orthodox answer to the problems of mankind. But man's redemption is one thing, and man's conduct in even a Christian society is quite another thing; the moralities were didactic where the moral interludes could allow humanist debate about the ideal behaviour of the scholar-gentleman of the Renaissance. Educational sociology was much in the air: Sir Thomas Elyot's *The Governor* had appeared in 1531, some thirty years before Hoby's translation of Castiglione's *Il Cortegiano*. The writers of the interludes were educated men interested in the new educational theories, and in their playlets there was always room for a pedagogical disquisition. Of John Rastell, for instance, Professor A. W. Reed wrote that his 'central position as the apostle of "natural reason and good philosophy" is the warp and weft of the interlude'.[2] The titles of some of these interludes are significant enough: *Wyt and Science*, *The Marriage of Wyt and Science*, *Nature*, *Witty and Witless*, *Gentleness and Nobility*. The authors were linked in family relationships as well as in interests; John Rastell, printer and disciple of Henry Medwall, was the brother-in-law of Sir Thomas More; and his son, William Rastell, was related by marriage to John Heywood, the greatest of the interlude writers, whose grandson (let bold literary genealogists make what they can of this fact!) was John Donne.

The debate of the two cultures, scholasticism and humanism, which is so frequently exemplified in the interlude, exemplifies also a curious duality of mind, a to-and-fro poise apparent also in the poets, whose deceptively 'simple' verse often displays in its uncertain reference a bewildered attempt at synthesis. This duality of mind has been expressed by a German academic critic as a

[1] Sylvia D. Feldman, *The Morality-Patterned Comedy of the Renaissance* (The Hague, 1971).
[2] The best discussion of the Medwall-Rastell group is to be found in A. W. Reed's *Early Tudor Drama* (1926), which is far more concerned with the More circle and the interlude than its rather general title would indicate.

'change in the driving-ideas, the transformation of prevailing symbols and slogans, and their content of new intellectual values [which] must be accurately traced and followed up in their static form as well as in their gradual development'.[1] A far more arresting description of this process is offered by Gertrude Stein (of all people) who, in some remarkable pages on English literary history, hits the nail bang on the head:

> In the whole of the Elizabethan literature . . . there is no confusion but there is a separation and to anyone doing it that is, writing, I am speaking of the Elizabethans to themselves inside them, there was this bother. And it was natural that there should be this bother . . . There was the daily island life and it made poetry and it made prose but there was also this separation and it made poetry and it made prose but the choice the choice was the thing. In a true daily island life the choice is not the thing. It was the outside separation that had come to be an inside separation, that made this thing. Think about it in any Elizabethan, any Elizabethan writing, in any Elizabethan who was writing. And words had everything to do with it . . .[2]

Not only in the larger issues of debate, but also in its more trivial moments the Tudor interlude was forensic throughout its whole structure, even to the point of absurd pedantry, as when in John Rastell's play of *Gentleness and Nobility* the pre-eminence of man over brute creation is solemnly discussed.[3] The Ploughman asks:

> Ys not yt the noblyst thyng in dede
> That of all other thynges hath lest nede
> As god which reynith etern in blysse
> Is not he the noblest thing yt is . . .
> . . . (because he) nedyth the helpe of no nother thyng
> To the helpe of his gloryous beyng
> But euery other thyng hath nede of his ayde.

[1] Konrad Burdach, *Reformation, Renaissance, Humanismus* (Berlin-Leipzig, 1926).
[2] Gertrude Stein, *Lectures in America* (N.Y., 1935).
[3] The quotations from *Gentleness and Nobility* are taken from A. W. Reed's *Early Tudor Drama*.

Back comes the Knight's retort that by this reasoning 'eurie beest fysse and other foule' is 'more noble of birth than a man',

> For man hath more nede of bodely couerying
> Than they haue for they nede no thinge
> The bestes haue herr & also a thick skin ...
> ... & so euri thing
> Bi nature hath his proper couering
> Saue man himself which is born all nakyd
> And therfore he shuld be than most wrechyd.

To which the Ploughman makes reply as follows:

> Yet this not wythstandyng
> Man is most noble of creatures lyuyng
> Not by hys body for that is impotent
> But for his soule beyng so excellent
> For by reason of his soule intellectyue
> He subdewyth all other bestis that be
> By his wit to releue his necessyte.

Moral dialogues in this form continued to be popular long after the slow decay of the interlude proper. Even as late as 1592, when Queen Elizabeth visited Quarendon in the Vale of Aylesbury during a royal progress, she was entertained, to quote the title of a section reprinted in *The Phoenix Nest*, by '*An Excellent Dialogue betweene Constancie and Inconstancie*, as it was by a speech presented to hir Majestie, in the last Progresse at Sir Henrie Leigh's house'.[1]

A short passage[2] of interlined speeches from Heywood's interlude of *The Pardoner and the Friar* will serve to show how much the comedy of these plays depended on closest attention to the spoken word. Here the two characters are carrying on two themes simultaneously, the appreciation of which must have made pretty strenuous demands on the court audience:

---

[1] The full entertainment is reprinted in R. W. Bond's edition of Lyly, to whom according to Rollins it is erroneously attributed (see his edition of *The Phoenix Nest*).

[2] *Dramatic Writings of John Heywood*, ed. J. S. Farmer (1905).

P. Pope Julius, Pope Innocent, with divers popes mo—
F. As the gospel full nobly doth declare—
P. Hath granted to the sustaining of the same—
F. How lived Epulus reigning in welfare—
P. Five thousand years of pardon to every of you by name—
F. And on his board dishes delicate—
P. And clean remission also of their sin—
F. Poor Lazarus came begging at his gate—
P. As often times as you put in—
F. Desiring some food his hunger to relieve—
P. Any money into the Pardoner's coffer—
F. But the rich man nothing would him give—
P. Or any money up unto it offer—
F. Not so much as a few crumbs of bread—
P. Or he that offreth penny or groat—
F. Wherefore poor Lazarus of famine straight was dead—
P. Or he that giveth the Pardoner a new coat—

and so on for lines. If these lines were delivered quickly, it must have taken a good deal of practice in the art of listening to keep the meanings apart, as well as to appreciate the ironies of juxtaposition, as for instance in the eleventh and twelfth lines of the passage quoted. That the audience was assumed to have this close interest is evident from the way in which they are frequently addressed directly by the characters as 'Masters!'

Thus the Tudor interlude is not only relevant in elucidating a debating tendency less explicitly stated in the better-known lyrics of the period; it helps also to explain the relationship between poet and reader. The court audience's habit of participation was to be transferred to the lyric, and later to the Elizabethan theatre as a reading and listening habit. The University Wits counted upon an audience which had been bred on moral rhetoric and was alert in attendance upon each sententious tag. Apprentices and housewives, like graduates from the two Universities as well as the worthy burghers of *The Knight of the Burning Pestle*, had all been brought up on 'sentences' in which formalized speech set forth various versions of formalized behaviour; the circle would be completed when the new plays passed the old saws back into circulation via the gallants who came to write down the choicest scraps into their table-books. The possibility of varying the tone of a play by transition from patterned speech to ordinary dialogue immeasurably extended the scope of the new dramatist. Of these habits of debate and of direct connection between performers and audience, Professor Bradbrook was able to say: 'Actually, the gradation between the frank appeal *ad spectatores* and the subtlest nuances of Shakespearean dramaturgy, make the dead-level of modern dialogue seem a very primitive affair.'[1]

The so-called tradition of courtly love and the morality-based debates of the moral interlude were but two instances of long-standing habits of open (sometimes banal) discussion of the individual's proper behaviour *vis-à-vis* his mistress, his church, his government, or ways of deceiving all three of them, which could be turned to account by the University Wits as readily as a modern playwright may count on 'audience participation' when he alludes to the moralizings of some well-known television personality or the serious questings of young men brought up on Freud and Marx. Alas, the one man among them who was really qualified to achieve great things with a truly argumentative dramatic Muse was denied the chance to utter a full challenge against the orthodoxy of his day. For when 'Christopherus Morley' was obscurely stabbed to death at Deptford Strand on May 30, 1593, there was removed from the Elizabethan scene the one man who, soundly versed in the classics and nourishing a truly English Renaissance re-activation of the classical spirit, yet active in the popular theatre and so in touch with contemporary idiom and popular echoes of medieval lore, might have brought the full intellectual stimulation of the New Learning into the mainstream of our dramatic literature. For Shakespeare, as Ben Jonson knew only too well, was not one of the University Wits; nor did he ever flourish with fine abandon those daring speculations—mocking, vigorous, 'atheistic', and joyfully ambitious—which in Marlowe give us a foretaste of the liberated energies of such later romantic literary heroes as Rimbaud or, in young Marlowe's more thoughtful moments, Albert Camus himself. Brooding over the records and

[1] M. C. Bradbrook, *Themes and Conventions of Elizabethan Tragedy* (1935).

E

achievements of Marlowe's life, one's thoughts fall into a doleful elegy. Spenser, drawing on the classics largely through Renaissance critics and emulators, helped classical pastoral to seduce the epic. Ben Jonson, after a struggle to bring the ancients to the Elizabethan stage, retired undefeated but unvictorious, and later helped to masque the drama. Christopher Marlowe, swimming the Hellespont between two worlds, died, like his own Leander, in midpassage.

V

The Paradox of Liberty in Shakespeare's England[1]

JOEL HURSTFIELD

WHEN, as a schoolboy, I began to read poetry for myself, I turned again and again to those lines and verses which brought the poet into the arena of politics. Even now, so long afterwards, I experience the same emotions as I did when I first read Wordsworth's lines:

> We must be free or die, who speak the tongue
> That Shakespeare spake. . . .[2]

I recall, too, Browning's famous rebuke of Wordsworth when he appeared to have abandoned the liberal cause:

> Shakespeare was of us, Milton was for us,
> Burns, Shelley were with us, they watch from their graves.[3]

Wordsworth, he cried, had deserted the noblest ideal of liberty with which the great poets had always been identified.

It is significant that, in the vanguard of these great liberal exponents, stands Shakespeare—or so, at least, Wordsworth, Browning and others always believed. I am not a literary critic but a historian; and one of the questions I have often been forced to ask myself about Shakespeare is: can we, in fact, include him among the great exponents of liberty, and did liberty mean very

[1] A revised version of the Shakespeare Birthday Lecture delivered at the Folger Shakespeare Library, Washington, in 1969. I am indebted to my colleague, Mr. Basil Greenslade, for reading and commenting on the text.

[2] *Poems dedicated to National Independence and Liberty*, Sonnet XVI (1803).

[3] 'The Lost Leader' (1845).

much to the society in which he lived? Did Elizabethan Englishmen understand the nature of individual liberty, did they want it,
do the plays of Shakespeare reflect these interests and aims? I shall
not anywhere say or imply that I know what Shakespeare himself
believed or wanted. But it is reasonable to hold a mirror up to
Shakespeare and see if he reflects to us any of the basic assumptions
of his age. In so doing I shall simply use Shakespeare as a historical
source, as I shall use other books and documents by contemporaries; and I shall try to extract from these difficult and ambiguous materials some idea of the concept of liberty in Shakespeare's
England. I shall also, in the final part of this paper, consider the
reflections of these sixteenth-century attitudes in modern English
society; and I shall ask why it is that, though we share a common
Shakespearean heritage, the role of liberty in American history is so
profoundly different from its historic role in England.

Liberty like beauty exists, I know, in the eye of the beholder.
We who earn our living, and pass much of our leisure, with the
written and spoken word believe that freedom of speech is the
highest currency. We consider that those who try to debase it are
the enemies of the common cultural heritage of the western world.
But the fervour with which we defend it should not obscure our
appreciation of the chequered story of its emergence. Liberty
of speech is not something that existed since time immemorial.
Nor was it often in the forefront of men's aims. When Milton
defended free speech in the middle of the seventeenth century he
spoke for a tiny minority. Cromwell and his followers didn't
believe in it; the Cavaliers certainly didn't believe in it; and the
vast mass of the people didn't care about it anyway. Liberty of
speech as an end in itself is of comparatively modern origin; I
doubt whether it is older than the eighteenth century. But since
then it has become part of our intellectual assumptions that freedom of speech is a fundamental and inalienable element in our
lives, that restraints upon this freedom threaten the very substance
of our world.

But there are many people in other places who do not share
what I loosely call these western intellectual traditions, and there

are many too in our society who have rejected them. They say that we are mistaking the part for the whole; that we over-rate freedom of speech and under-rate the other freedoms, freedom from want, freedom from false materialist values, freedom from the power of an entrenched minority. They say, too, that starving men would readily sacrifice liberty of speech for a square meal under an autocratic government.[1]

I draw attention to these criticisms not because I accept them but because they are made by a large number of sincere and able people and their governments in many parts of the world, and because they are supported by a formidable mass of evidence about the nature and extent of our freedom and about the agencies which mould opinion in a free western society. But, apart from this, I draw attention to these attitudes because it makes it easier for us to understand that Shakespeare's contemporaries could also dispense with our modern intellectual assumptions about liberty, though for reasons quite different from those of our modern critics.

But before I come to my central theme, I want to make clear that I am concerned with liberty, not independence, which is an entirely different thing. It is the confusion of these two ideals which has put Shakespeare, mistakenly in my view, among the founding fathers of the modern liberal outlook. Throughout modern history, in the overwhelming majority of cases, the movement for national independence has preceded the belief in individual liberty; and it is independence not liberty which figures so prominently in many of Shakespeare's plays. The sense of nationalism, already marked in fifteenth-century England, and vastly enlarged by the English Reformation under Henry VIII, came to its full flowering in the age of Shakespeare. It is in the sixteenth century that England ceased to be an offshore island lying to the north-west of Europe, and became instead an Atlantic power aware and proud of her nationhood, jealous of her independence:

[1] 'Most people still measure freedom,' observed Khrushchev, 'in terms of how much meat, how many potatoes, or what kind of boots they can get for one rouble.'

> This royal throne of kings, this sceptred isle,
> This earth of majesty, this seat of Mars,
> This other Eden, demi-paradise,
> This fortress built by Nature for herself... (*Ric. II*, II. i. 40–3)

These are familiar words, every schoolboy knows them. But if it is true that these lines could only have been written by Shakespeare, it is also true that they could only have been written in the sixteenth century.

Henceforth those twenty-two miles of water which separate England from the continental land mass became less a channel of communication in a common culture and religion, and more a moat preserving England against European pressure during the time of English imperial expansion overseas, on the American continent and beyond. It is only in the present generation that the process has been reversed and England, turning away at last from anachronistic concepts of empire, has begun to resume her role as an integrated member of a European society.

With national independence I am not concerned on this occasion; though it would be fruitful to inquire why in Shakespeare's plays there is so much which evokes the highest emotions of national independence and so little which proclaims the glories of personal freedom. But it is personal freedom which we must here consider; and I turn first from Shakespeare's plays to Shakespeare's countrymen.

Freedom implies government by consent and, therefore, the right to dissent. It implies the right to say, write, and do what I please, in order to accomplish what I seek, provided that I do not use force or the threat of force to achieve my purposes. If, however, my critics can prove that my words or deeds can do positive harm, my freedom of speech or action will be reduced or even withdrawn. To this extent I live under restraint. But my freedom is not only limited in this way. I have given up other things as well. I cannot control all my income because some of it I must give up as taxation. I cannot build a house where I like nor can I even control the house in which I live because, if the government decides to build a six-lane motorway over the land on which it stands, and is unwilling to make a detour to suit my convenience, they will pull my house down, give me a sum of money and tell me to go and live elsewhere. In these, and in many other ways, I have lost some part of my freedom; yet this is a situation which, however reluctantly, I accept. I do so because I believe that the society I live in is based on consent. By consent I mean not simply the right to put in —or, more likely, throw out—the government every five years. I mean much more: I mean the right to organize movements, parties, demonstrations, protests; the right to speak and publish what I please in defence of my interests or ideals. It means, in short, the continuous exercise of my right to inquire and to dissent. For, if I have not the publicly recognized right to *dissent*, then my nominal *consent* at elections is a mockery of the term.

Since consent is central to my theme, I ask whether Shakespeare's contemporaries consented to the government which ruled over them. We are fortunate in that one of these contemporaries commented on this very question in his study of the society and government of his day. Sir Thomas Smith, scholar, politician, civil servant, ambassador to France, sets before us, in a famous passage in his book, *De Republica Anglorum*, a detailed description of parliamentary authority and procedure. He tells us that matters are debated and issues are decided in the two Houses of Parliament. Bills which have been approved, and have received the royal assent, become law. 'Anything there enacted,' writes his contemporary William Harrison, 'is not to be misliked but obeyed of all men without contradiction or grudge.' This is taken as the voice of the whole nation, for all men are represented there.[1]

But every Tudor historian knows that this was the *form* of authority and that real power lay elsewhere. He knows that only a fraction of the population had the suffrage and that, in any case, elections rarely took place. The results in the county seats were, in the overwhelming majority of cases, agreed upon—or as we should say, fixed—by the leading families in the county; in the boroughs elections were usually determined by an oligarchy, or

[1] Sir Thomas Smith, *De Republica Anglorum*, ed. L. Alston (Camb., 1906) pp. 48 ff.; W. Harrison, *Description of England*, ed. G. Edelen (Folger Shakespeare Library (Ithaca, 1968)), pp. 149 ff.

by a single patron. Some four hundred members were 'elected' in this way, and they were drawn from a narrow sector in the upper ranges of society; while the members of the House of Lords went through no process of election whatsoever. Moreover, years went by without Parliament being summoned at all so its average duration during the reign of Elizabeth I—as Sir John Neale has shown —was three weeks each year.[1] Its powers too could be neutralized by the government in quashing bills or with other devices; and it could be shut down altogether at short notice by the crown. In any case, a large area of the national interest was held to be outside parliamentary debate or decision.

The more we examine the procedure of consent, the more it is reduced to the limited processes of minority rule. For the men who consented in Parliament, if elected at all, were sent there by a small section of the total community and themselves belonged to a smaller section of those who had elected them. Yet they believed that they had the right to consent on behalf of the nation as a whole, as Sir Thomas Smith said they had; and here was a fundamental distinction between them and us. Smith and his contemporaries held that a man could represent his community by virtue of his station in life. This concept was the product of medieval feudalism and Tudor paternalism. A member of parliament consented on behalf of his community much as a father consents on behalf of his family. Neither was elected by those on whose behalf he consented. But to us representation in Parliament is taken to include *election* and we assume that without election no man can claim to represent his community. Yet we forget how recently this has come about. Just over fifty years ago no woman in England had the vote. It was assumed that her views were adequately represented by her husband or some other consenting male. In most other countries until recently large sections of the population had no part in the election. But their consent was assumed. In Tudor England the same assumption was made. Power of consent was vested in a much smaller segment of society than today and the representatives owed their powers to their wealth, their social standing and their birth.

[1] J. E. Neale, *The Elizabethan House of Commons* (1949), pp. 381 and 433.

Consent then, freedom of election, functioned only within these constitutional restraints. But there were other controls as well. We now understand better than we once did the marvellous power which an efficient propaganda machine can exercise on behalf of the state or an individual interest; and such a propaganda machine existed in Tudor England. Before the middle of the sixteenth century the printing press had been harnessed to the political aims of government.[1] Thomas Cromwell quickly learned to exploit it: the pamphlet and the pulpit gave a measure of influence over men's minds and judgments which added a new dimension to the organs of control. Royal progresses played their part too, and so did proclamations, as did what we should call the 'briefing' of the county leaders at quarter sessions and the assizes. This is not to say that these measures always succeeded: printer or preacher might take an independent line. But if they did there were heavy sanctions to be called into play. For the one John Stubbes, who lost a hand in the service of political dissent, there were many printers and preachers who did what they were told. For the one Peter Wentworth who sacrificed his liberty in a defiant gesture for freedom of speech there were many other members of parliament who sat silently on their benches in Westminster, or, indeed, vainly counselled him to put a rein on his eloquence.[2]

I have argued so far that the Tudor conception of consent was (at least in theory) different from our own; and, secondly, that the kind of liberty that a twentieth-century writer regards as the *sine qua non* of his very existence figures only rarely in the works of Shakespeare's contemporaries. His greatest contemporary, Francis Bacon, enlarged his collection of essays from ten in 1597 to thirty-eight in 1612, to fifty-eight in 1625. They covered an ever-widening spectrum of human affairs, including Truth, Death, Atheism, Empire, Counsel, The True Greatness of Kingdoms, Usury, Faction, Judicature, and many other large and fundamental issues. Yet he left us no essay on Liberty. When we meet

[1] See e.g., W. G. Zeeveld, *Foundations of Tudor Policy* (1948); Frances A. Yates, 'Queen Elizabeth as Astraea', *Journal of Warburg and Courtauld Inst.* X (1947), pp. 27–82.

[2] J. E. Neale, *Elizabeth I and her Parliaments, 1584–1601* (1957), pp. 154 ff. and *passim*.

the word in Shakespeare's plays we meet it usually in the narrow sense of being set at liberty from prison, or in the more technical sense of privilege, the medieval notion of *libertas*, as indeed it is used in Magna Carta. But when Shakespeare uses the word liberty in a sense nearest our own, it is heavily loaded with irony, scepticism and the deliberate assumption that liberty, licence and mob rule are close companions in political unrest. 'Liberty,' says the Duke in *Measure for Measure*, 'plucks justice by the nose' (I. iii. 29); but the implications of the passage are ambiguous. But there is no ambiguity in the famous scene in *2 Henry VI* where Jack Cade, leader of the rebels, addresses his henchmen:

> And you that love the commons follow me.
> Now show yourselves men; 'tis for liberty.
> We will not leave one lord, one gentleman;
> Spare none but such as go in clouted shoon. (IV. ii. 178–81)

And then, in the next scene, after the savage battle on Blackheath, Cade congratulates Dick, the butcher of Ashford, on his share in the slaughter:

> They fell before thee like sheep and oxen, and thou behavedst thyself as if thou hadst been in thine own slaughter-house.

Shortly after, Cade adds:

> the bodies shall be dragged at my horse heels till I do come to London, where we will have the mayor's sword borne before us . . . (IV. iii. 3 ff.)

This harsh picture of the rebels who murder in the name of liberty is not unexpected, for the peasant wars of Reformation Europe, quite apart from England's experience of more modest affairs, formed part of the folk-inheritance of the age. But in *Julius Caesar* it is not the peasantry but members of the governing class who wage battle for liberty. We notice that after the murder of Caesar, it is Cinna who utters the battle-cry:

> Liberty! Freedom! Tyranny is dead!
> Run hence, proclaim, cry it about the streets;

And it is Cassius who reinforces him with:

> Some to the common pulpits, and cry out,
> Liberty, freedom and enfranchisement!

Brutus at first is slow to respond. He uses none of the conspirators' rhetoric but introduces a note of calm:

> People and Senators, be not affrighted;
> Fly not; stand still. Ambition's debt is paid.

But then, under pressure, he responds, and strikes the same note as his fellows. He bids men to bathe their hands and swords in Caesar's blood:

> And waving our red weapons o'er our heads
> Let's all cry, 'Peace, freedom and liberty!' (III. i. 78 ff.)

Here surely is the moment of supreme irony: peace proclaimed in the market place with a bloody sword!

When we meet liberty in Shakespeare we meet it in the responding company of violence. I mention these incidents merely to indicate that, though poets like Wordsworth or Browning may have found in Shakespeare an ally in freedom's cause, a mere historian finds the search for liberty in this context difficult and unrewarding. This difficulty arises, I think, because of the relationship between liberty and equality. Freedom of speech and organization depends, among other things, on the principle that men have equal rights. (I am not speaking of the doctrine that all men are created equal, which is another matter, and I shall come to this shortly.) If men have equal rights in the sight of the law, then they have equal rights to say and write what they please, subject of course to the equal rights of other men, as I have already indicated. But Shakespeare's England was not based on equal rights, and least of all on any conception of human equality. Magna Carta, it is true, had long ago declared that all freemen had equal rights before the law, but 'freeman' was a technical term and it extended to only a proportion of the people. By the sixteenth century Magna Carta was in any case rarely referred to save by antiquarian political radicals: Shakespeare managed to write his play *King John* without a single mention of it. Englishmen did not regard all men as equal in any sense of the word. They did not even believe that men had equal rights to wear certain kinds of clothes—there was legislation to stop humble folk from aping the dress of the rich[1]—let alone regard men as having equal rights to make speeches or write pamphlets. The Speaker of the House of Commons in his formal request for freedom of speech at the opening of the session always stopped well short of any such request. Tudor society, by any measure, was an unequal society.

In place of equality there existed hierarchy. It is impossible to understand the Tudor way of life—or for that matter a good deal of Tudor literature—without seeing it as a society based on order and degree. I need not cite here the long speech of Ulysses in Shakespeare's *Troilus and Cressida*, where the virtues of this kind of social structure are vigorously expounded. I turn instead to his contemporary, William Harrison, who in his *Description of England* has a section called 'Of Degrees of People in the Commonwealth of England'. Here is clearly brought out the nature of an aristocratic, articulated society, with the orders of nobility and knighthood, followed by esquires, gentlemen, yeomen, citizens, husbandmen, artificers, and on to idle servingmen and beggars. And, according to Harrison, each man more or less knows his place.[2] This is, of course, looking at the world through rose-tinted, conservative spectacles. But it was a commonly expressed view.

Hierarchy was the cement of the existing order. It belonged, as Professor Lovejoy and others have argued, to a cosmic concept of

---

[1] E.g., F. E. Baldwin, *Sumptuary Legislation and Personal Regulation in England*, Chapters IV and V. For a recent discussion of this problem see the work of my pupil Joan R. Kent, 'Social attitudes of Members of Parliament with special reference to the Problem of Poverty, c.1590–1624' (unpublished London Ph.D. thesis, 1970), Chapter 7.

[2] W. Harrison, *Description of England*, Chapter V.

the Great Chain of Being, reaching in harmony and order from the godhead to the humblest element in the universe.[1] It was part of a divine logic into which every fragment of life could be fitted. Whether Englishmen of Shakespeare's day were as aware of the Great Chain of Being as are Harvard undergraduates of today who study Shakespeare, I don't really know. Recent scholarship has brought out the complexity and variety of the contemporary responses to these 'assumptions'.[2] But the common opinion was that this was a stratified society and that so it should remain. Men like Lord Burghley, the principal minister of Queen Elizabeth— the Polonius of Hamlet—saw perfectly well that there was a gap between theory and practice: many men did not remain in the station in which they were born. Burghley himself did not. This was a fairly fluid society with a certain amount of social mobility, too much in the opinion of great conservatives like Burghley and the queen. And like all conservatives they tried to pretend that nothing had happened.

Hierarchy preserved and justified the framework of an unequal society. Popularity threatened it. Popularity meant an appeal to the people, to popular opinion: in essence to call in liberty to threaten order. Francis Bacon warned the Earl of Essex against seeking popular support.[3] 'I love the people'—we turn again to the Duke in *Measure for Measure*:

> But do not like to stage me to their eyes;
> Though it do well, I do not relish well
> Their loud applause and Aves vehement;
> Nor do I think the man of safe discretion
> That does affect it. (I. i. 68 ff.)

One recalls at this point the revulsion of Coriolanus as he enters Rome and is given a hero's welcome by the crowds:

[1] A. O. Lovejoy, *The Great Chain of Being: a study of the history of an idea* (Camb. Mass., 1936); E. M. W. Tillyard, *The Elizabethan World Picture* (1948).

[2] W. Sanders, *The Dramatist and the Received Idea: Studies in the Plays of Marlowe and Shakespeare* (1968).

[3] *The Letters and the Life of Francis Bacon*, ed. J. Spedding (1862), ii. 44.

> No more of this, it does offend my heart;
> Pray now, no more. (II. i. 159–60)

Burghley, drawing up a code of behaviour for a rising politician, that is to say his son, Robert Cecil, thought that it might be possible to strike a happy mean: 'I advise thee not to affect nor neglect popularity too much. Seek not to be E and shun to be R.'[1] Any consideration of Shakespeare as a historical source for the political thinking of his age—and I emphasize again that this is not taken to mean that Shakespeare himself held these views—must have special regard to *Coriolanus*. For here again and again are raised fundamental questions about the character and legitimacy of popular rule. Coriolanus himself rejects all notion that the people have any right to govern, or indeed any claim to be flattered. But quite apart from his extreme position, the play itself provides a contrast between aristocratic rule, in the form of patricians and senators, and popular pressures expressed through the people and their tribunes. To the nobility popular rule is an affront to reason. Coriolanus' mother is said to regard the people as

> woollen vassals, things created
> To buy and sell with groats; to show bare heads
> In congregations, to yawn, be still and wonder,
> When one but of my ordinance stood up
> To speak of peace or war. (III. ii. 9 ff.)

But even the more tolerant Menenius speaks of them in bitter scorn:

> ... you and your apron men; you that stood so much
> Upon the voice of occupation and
> The breath of garlic-eaters! (IV. vi. 97 ff.)[2]

---

[1] *Advice to a Son*, ed. L. B. Wright (Folger Shakespeare Library (Ithaca, 1962)), p. 13. The initials are normally taken to stand for Essex and Raleigh.

[2] See also W. G. Zeeveld, '"Coriolanus" and Jacobean Politics', *The Modern Language Review* (1962), l.vii. 321–34.

Anyone who reads Thomas Smith on government with his clear, firm and elaborate account of parliamentary election and voting finds a harsh parody of it in Coriolanus' ironical appeal ('voice' is the sixteenth-century word for 'vote'):

> Your voices! For your voices I have fought;
> Watched for your voices; for your voices bear
> Of wounds two dozen odd; battles thrice six
> I have seen and heard of; for your voices have
> Done many things, some less, some more. Your voices!
>   (II. iii. 123 ff.)

We cannot fail to notice the effect of mounting irony by repetition of the word 'voices'.

Everything that I have said so far indicates that this was an unequal society. If we want to grasp the sentiments of Shakespeare's Englishman we should, in effect, put from our minds the language of Wordsworth and Browning. We might usefully turn instead to a Victorian hymn; a hymn which was still being sung at school when I was a boy but which, I imagine, if suggested now, would lead to fighting in the streets:

> The rich man in his castle,
> The poor man at his gate,
> God made them high or lowly,
> And ordered their estate.

And ordered their estate. For long, if with diminishing confidence, the Elizabethans clung to this comforting conviction, until their world crumbled beneath them.

Hierarchy to our modern minds is rightly associated with rigidity, privilege and an ingrained hostility to change. Much of this indeed applies to the men who governed England in the sixteenth century. But if we use the term only in its pejorative sense we lose a great deal of the texture of English life of those days. For, if it was an aristocratic society, this was an aristocracy assumed to be responsible for the community over which it exercised its privilege. Some of these noblemen, it is true, were no more than harsh and selfish power-seekers or drunken idlers, some of the gentry brutal, quarrelsome adherents of faction. Yet built into this ruling order was an element of responsibility, forced on them often by the central government, yet inherited too with their lands and their titles. *Noblesse oblige*: I have to turn to a French expression to convey this complex of attitudes which characterized the best elements—but only the best elements—of the English governing class. Put briefly, their wealth and their position were regarded as imposing a trust, a trust conferred upon them to serve the public interest, the welfare of the whole nation. In some respects Lord Burghley tried to follow this ideal. So did the Earl of Huntingdon, so did Sir Nicholas Bacon, father of the philosopher, so did many members of parliament, so did leading citizens and gentry whose deeds we now dimly see in the faded and obscure records of local administration. The pamphlet literature of the late sixteenth century, the parliamentary speeches, the sermons contain, it is true, much in them that is shallow, harsh, couched in that self-righteous language beloved of men in any age who defend their own vested interests. But when that is said, there remains a good deal in both the literature and the legislation of the period which reaches forward, to a surprising degree, to the social thinking of the nineteenth and twentieth centuries.

This then was the unequal society of sixteenth-century England. It was a place where the publication of political or religious dissent was not permitted; where the practice of the Catholic faith was prohibited; where there were restraints on what men read, what they ate—on Fish Days—what they bought, what they sold, where they travelled. Where in all this, we may ask, was liberty? In every age there are a few men who glimpse all the rich prospects of liberty and seek to preserve it, whatever the cost. Erasmus of Rotterdam came nearer than other men to an understanding of the nature and value of individual freedom. Our own Thomas More as a young man may have held similar views, if *Utopia* is any guide to his thinking; but in this case a combination of middle age and politics—as ever the twin sources of disillusion—quenched his ardour. The Elizabethan member of parliament, Peter Wentworth, spoke divinely and courageously about liberty, and had some understanding of it in his own cantankerous way. But it was not theory which preserved some measure of liberty in Shakespeare's England. Rather it was the government's unwillingness—and more often its inability—to implement the legislation. The anti-Catholic laws were on many occasions not enforced, sometimes on the instruction of the queen; there was likewise a toleration of Puritans in high places. And a good deal of literature hostile to the most eminent men of the day managed to circulate widely. I don't want to suggest for one moment that the queen and her government presided benignly over the widespread expression of diversity of opinion. It did nothing of the kind: it hated criticism and did its best to repress it.

I have come over the years reluctantly to the conclusion that the measure of private freedom in Shakespeare's England was small; that the government tried where it could to condition men's minds and, where it could not, to repress diversity of opinion. It did so because it believed that any challenge to its interests or the existing social structure threatened the future order and stability of England. It did so because it was deeply fearful of a restoration of Catholicism in England and therefore submission—so it seemed —to a foreign power. Alternatively, dissent might lead to a Puritan struggle, civil war and a weakened England, occupied by a foreign power. In short, it thought that to preserve social stability and national freedom it must suppress private freedom. This is the recurrent paradox of liberty in the history of the western world from the Reformation to the present day.

But there is a difference between the history of Tudor England and that of most European countries. It was a hierarchic society as was theirs, but in the course of Shakespeare's lifetime there was built into hierarchy the responsibility for making the welfare legislation effective; and both legislation and hierarchy survived. I argue that where a governing class—I mean a class, not just the government—is committed to, and involved in, the welfare of the whole society, there is relative stability; and where there is stability some measure of liberty can survive. But where a governing class is not so committed there is alienation, the divisions harden,

F

distrust leads to violence, and where violence determines the issue, we get extreme fluctuations; for governing bodies in their weakness yield everything to force and, when they recover their strength, take all back and repression prevails. In the process true liberty perishes.

Social stability preserved some elements of liberty, and provided the conditions in which liberty could grow; but it was not that alone. And here we find a curiously contradictory element in the system of government. For, though liberty was restrained, enough of it survived to challenge hierarchy itself. Or, to put it another way, neither monarchy nor aristocracy was allowed to harden into supremacy, rigidity and isolation. They never, as it were, emancipated themselves from their human condition. This was a class system, not a caste system. Nowhere is this better brought out than in the plays of Shakespeare. He appears at one and the same time to accept and reject the divine attributes of kingship, to accept and reject the hierarchic system of the Elizabethans.

The crown is separate, anointed, divine, but the king is also a man. Henry V, walking in disguise on the night before Agincourt, explains to three soldiers that the king has all the ordinary qualities of a man:

> The violet smells to him as it does to me; the element shows to him as it doth to me; all his senses have but human conditions; his ceremonies laid by, in his nakedness he appears but a man . . . (IV. i. 103 ff.)

In his soliloquy after the soldiers have gone he reverts to the same thought:

> And what have kings that privates have not too,
> Save ceremony—save general ceremony?
> And what art thou, thou idol Ceremony? . . .
> O Ceremony, show me but thy worth!
> What is thy soul of Adoration?
> Art thou aught else but place, degree and form?
> (IV. i. 234 ff.)

The king, when all is considered, is a man as are other men, but to him falls the pomp and burden of royalty:

> the balm, the sceptre, and the ball
> The sword, the mace, the crown imperial,
> The intertissued robe of gold and pearl. (IV. i. 256 ff.)

In this, as in so much in Shakespeare, the universal man denies the inequality affirmed in form and ritual; just as in *The Merchant of Venice* his Shylock breaks through for a moment the hierarchy of race and religions.

We are, as it were, looking at Shakespeare's England on two levels: the elaborate order of artifice which is clearly visible to the naked eye, and below it the rough, hard surface of reality scarred and cracked under the dissolving pressures of change.

It may be that this tension between things as they seemed and things as they were helps us to explain such violence as existed in Tudor England—I do not mean civil war but the sporadic street violence, the quick exchange of blows, the swift hand to the dagger, the vendettas of feuding groups over an acre of disputed land or some imagined insult. When we read of the splendours of Elizabethan culture and achievement it is of interest to recall that a man might spend the evening in one of the great houses of London holding subtle discourse on literature, or listening to the most exquisite music, yet, if he ventured out at night alone, half a mile from that very house in the capital city of England he might have his purse stolen, his head broken, and count himself fortunate to escape with his life. The contemporary who, as poet and playwright, was second only to Shakespeare was killed at the age of thirty in a violent incident in a tavern. What, I have sometimes asked myself, did the audience feel as they listened to the almost unspeakable horror and bestiality of *Titus Andronicus?* I do not myself believe that this experience can be explained—or explained away—by the time-honoured *cliché* of *catharsis*. It is rather a reflection of the dualism in society, the conflict between form and reality, between power and the limitations upon its exercise. In the course of this conflict liberty was preserved.

If we can see this dualism reflected in Shakespeare's plays, we can see it more clearly in the contemporary politics. The courtier Earl of Essex, the perfect image of the gallant nobleman reared to the mystique of royalty, wrote thus in 1598 to the Lord Keeper of the Great Seal: 'I owe to Her Majesty the duty of an Earl and Lord Marshall of England.' But, he said, he was being demeaned from his high place to the position of a slave. And now, in the moment of truth, he tore away the enveloping illusion of an infallible crown:

> What, cannot princes err? Cannot subjects receive wrong? Is an earthly power or authority infinite? Pardon me, pardon me, my good Lord; I can never subscribe to these principles.[1]

This was blunt and crude, and was written at a time of great personal strain. But it had been said with greater eloquence yet equal vigour more than twenty years earlier by that most troublesome member of parliament, Peter Wentworth:

> Certain it is, Mr. Speaker, that none is without fault: no, not our noble Queen ... It is a dangerous thing in a Prince unkindly to intreat and abuse his or her nobility and people, as Her Majesty did the last Parliament. And it is a dangerous thing in a Prince to oppose or bend herself against her nobility and people.[2]

John Knox's views about the authority of James VI of Scotland and about James' mother, Mary Queen of Scots, as well as about Mary Tudor of England, are too well-known to be recalled at this time.

The Rev. Edward Dering, in a famous sermon preached before the Queen of England in 1570, rebuked her for allowing a grave decline in the quality of the Anglican church which, he said, now included among its ministers 'some shake bucklers, some ruffians,

---

[1] W. B. Devereux, *Lives and Letters of the Devereux, Earls of Essex* (1853), i. 501.

[2] J. E. Neale, *Elizabeth I and her Parliaments, 1559–1581* (1953), p. 322.

some hawkers and hunters, some dicers and carders, some blind guides and cannot see, some dumb dogs and will not bark'. And thus he addressed her sovereign majesty:

> And yet you in the meanwhile that all these whoredoms are committed, you at whose hands God will require it, you sit still and are careless, let men do as they list. It toucheth not belike your commonwealth, and therefore you are so well contented to let all alone.[1]

What was said about kings was said, too, about archbishops and noblemen. The ordered hierarchy was under challenge. If Peter Wentworth had no hesitation in rebuking an archbishop, the Rev. Thomas Wood had none about writing in the frankest possible terms to eminent statesmen like William Cecil, the Earl of Leicester, and his brother, the Earl of Warwick. We may take simply as illustration the opening of one such letter from Wood to the Earl of Warwick:

> Many very ill and dishonourable brutes (Right Honourable and my singular good Lord) are spread abroad of my Lord your brother, which I do oft hear to my great grief.

Wood goes on to criticize Leicester's handling of religious matters and to add, too, a reference to his private life; and, he ends, if these rumours are true, 'God's judgments in the opinion of all godly men without speedy repentance is not far off, and therefore had need to be plainly dealt withall.'[2]

You will have noticed that the critics I have cited—and they are drawn from a much larger number—had one thing in common: they were Puritans. And it is this which provides us with our principal clue to the rapid collapse of the ordered society of the Elizabethans. Everyone knows that the Puritan movement, with

[1] P. Collinson, *A Mirror of Elizabethan Puritanism*, Friends of Dr. Williams' Library, 17th Lecture (1964), p. 17.

[2] *Letters of Thomas Wood, Puritan, 1566–1577*, ed. P. Collinson (Special supplement, No. 5, *Bull. of Inst. Hist. Research*, 1960), pp. 9 ff.

its increasing moral commitment to austerity, constituted a threat to English drama and to culture as a whole. Its threat to the state was more enduring because it was fundamental. For here was a basic clash in authority. The Tudor sovereigns owed their power to the long traditions of monarchy, to their supremacy in the church and to the semi-divine qualities with which anointing endowed them. The Puritans were prepared to recognize the sovereign as head of the church and state, but they acknowledged an authority greater than the monarch: the voice of God as made known to man in the Bible. The rediscovering of the Bible by the Puritans— it was no less—has perhaps not always been given its fullest weight by historians. For the Puritans were perhaps the first Christian sect to use the Old Testament as the Jews did, not simply as a religious source but as a code of private and public behaviour. Here they lighted upon the Sabbath in its primitive form with results which are still familiar to this day to anyone who cares to spend a wet Sunday in Edinburgh or Philadelphia. In the Bible also they entered upon a world which was without bishops, and for long periods without kings. And they found, too, that when there were kings who sinned or were in error, they were corrected or deposed by a righteous God acting through the agency of his chosen people. So, armed with the knowledge of God acting through history, the Puritans challenged the bishops, the monarch and, in effect, the existing order. 'Let them,' said the Earl of Essex to the Lord Keeper in the letter I have already cited, 'acknowledge an infinite absoluteness on earth that do not believe in an absolute infiniteness in Heaven.'[1]

Still more important for our purpose, the Puritans rediscovered a spiritual world without hierarchy, as had Luther and the other Protestants who followed him, a world in which all men were equal in the sight of God. But Luther had always believed that this equality began and ended in Heaven and had nothing to do with the kingdoms of this world. The Anabaptists had gone further and sought to establish equality on earth, at once and in all material as well as spiritual things, with a consequent reign of terror first by them and then to suppress them. The Puritans were not

---

[1] W. B. Devereux, op. cit., i. 501 ff.

communists as the Anabaptists were. Few of them ever dreamed of the equal ownership of wealth and power. They still envisaged social inequality and held that the 'magistrates', the *élite*, should act for the people as a whole. But at least the basis of their system was popular, and the monarch, like themselves, was under the law. And they demanded freedom to speak their minds.

This was an erosive doctrine; and it was already possible to see during the last decade of Shakespeare's life, when the Tudors had given place to the Stuarts, that the Puritans and their parliamentary allies were unwilling to acknowledge the divine right of the existing order. This alone could not have destroyed Charles I. Rather it was blunders on both sides, intolerance, and, in the end, deep distrust of a king who would lie and twist to his subjects provided that he was faithful to the higher authority of God: all these brought civil war and the execution of Charles I in 1649.

But I have left out one important ingredient in this process of dissolution. I refer to the printing press. The long-term effects of the invention of printing in the middle of the fifteenth century were, and still are, ambiguous. Most sixteenth-century governments, including that of England, used it as an instrument of control, by means of pamphlets, proclamations, homilies and other devices. But the voice of dissent used the printing press too, sometimes, as in the famous case of the Marprelate tracts, an itinerant, clandestine press, until it was captured and smashed up by the government. But others appeared, or foreign printers were called to the service of a worthy cause. Our heavily indented coastline, and our proximity to the continent of Europe, meant that there was no effective barrier against a small boat bringing dangerous truths to the faithful. Freedom found an ally in the printer.

All these various forces pressed upon and cracked the constitutional mould of the Stuart government. For a time it was set aside as irreparable, and the Puritans, under the Protector Oliver Cromwell, held power. But, while a minority of his followers held passionately to the doctrine of equality, though not of personal freedom, neither the Protector nor his parliamentarians found it viable or indeed desirable. Hence the government of Cromwell moved back to hierarchy and came to resemble in form, but not formalities, the government of the Stuarts. Hence the logic of the situation called for a return of the Stuarts. Things were never the same again, and there was a further revolution a generation later. But the Puritans had failed; the old social order, the old complex social hierarchy, resumed its place and function.

And here is one more paradox in this strange story. Had the Puritans triumphed, they might have built up a formidable apparatus of repression; and the slender shoots of liberty could have been crushed back into the soil. But they were neither strong enough to win nor weak enough, even in defeat, to be discounted. They survived, a permanent, nonconformist movement which grew in dignity, integrity, idealism and in its demands for freedom. Greater in defeat than in victory, they passed on to succeeding generations, and in many unexpected guises, the liberal outlook which the nonconformist conscience—at its best—has contributed to the world.

But though the Puritans failed in England they lived to fight the battle anew overseas. To follow this battle, I must make an excursion into American history. Shakespeare's *Tempest* depicts for us a new world free from the encrusted traditions of the old. For many English dissenters, Puritan and Catholic alike, such a new world was, in Shakespeare's lifetime, already in the making. Four years before *The Tempest* was first produced, English colonists had made a successful settlement in Virginia, a settlement which endures to this day. And in *The Tempest* we encounter the first, and purest, version of the American dream:

Had I the plantation of this isle, my Lord,

says Gonzalo, and then, ignoring ribald interruptions, he goes on:

I' the commonwealth I would by contraries
Execute all things; for no kind of traffic
Would I admit; no name of magistrate;
Letters should not be known; riches, poverty,
And use of service, none; contract, succession,
Bourn, bound of land, tilth, vineyard, none;

No use of metal, corn, or wine, or oil;
No occupation; all men idle, all;
And women too, but innocent and pure;
No sovereignty. (II. i. 137 ff.)

No sovereignty. Here at last would be cast off the long, burdensome traditions and organization, and men would be as free as the air they breathed. The paradox of liberty and order would be resolved, or rather, it would become irrelevant. The passage is full of irony and satire but it had certain qualities of the ever-recurring American dream.

We are told that when Moses took the Children of Israel out of Egypt he caused them to tarry for forty years in the wilderness so that the generation which reached the promised land would have shed all memories of subjection and of an older order. For the American colonists, though they endured on the Atlantic many stormy weeks in their long, courageous, hazardous passage from the old world to the new, the time was not long enough. They brought with them, and re-established, many of the institutions and attitudes of their forefathers. But not all. The Puritan vein was stronger in many of them than in the people they had left behind; and it was enduring. And when, after a century and a half, they rejected once and for all the old dominion, and established a republic, they rejected also not only monarchy but the whole conception of hierarchy.

'We hold these truths to be self evident: that all men are created equal.' Now the Americans possessed a doctrine which the British have never had, before or since, the doctrine of the equality of man. English people were prepared to believe that all men are equal in the sight of God. They came in time to believe that they were equal in the sight of the law. They came in time to seek to get nearer to equality of opportunity. But the equality of man they have never affirmed.

The English had deposed Charles I, but they summoned back Charles II. The Americans deposed George III, but they never restored George IV. Behind this symbolic difference in our histories lies the fundamental difference in our societies. And three generations later, in the time of another great upheaval, Abraham Lincoln turned back to the hallowed sources of American freedom:

Four score and seven years ago our fathers brought forth on this continent a new nation, conceived in Liberty, and dedicated to the proposition that all men are created equal.

Here was the clear identification of equality with liberty, a commitment to equality which the best of every succeeding American generation has acknowledged as binding upon itself. Here, too, I think lies part of the explanation of the troubled conscience of modern America; but that is another story.

With us the chain of events was different. Our Bill of Rights of 1689 was a negative thing: it laid down what the king might not in future do. But the doctrine of equality is never visible in its clauses. For the seventeenth century, like time past and time future, was an age of inequality. Yet liberty was somehow preserved. How did this come about? If liberty is allied with equality, it is also allied with security. For it is only when men feel secure that they move freely and speak freely: and this freedom Englishmen increasingly enjoyed from Shakespeare's day until ours, in fact rather than in form. They owed it to a complex of historical causes; and we have a pre-vision of the essential framework of stability in Elizabethan England. For, by the end of the sixteenth century, Englishmen were coming to see that violence was the product of instability, and that instability derived in part from poverty. In the second half of the sixteenth century the local authorities and the central government moved unevenly, reluctantly towards a programme of alleviating unemployment and ameliorating the effects of sickness and old age. The Poor Law Act of 1598, consolidating the experience of more than half a century, set out the main objectives of the welfare legislation which was to survive in England for two and a half centuries. Some, looking to its past, would call the policy interested paternalism, that is, paternalism in the interest of the governing classes; others, looking to the future, could regard it as the blue-print of a welfare state. Whatever it was, it gave to

England a larger measure of stability, and therefore the promise of freedom, than was given to other nations in Europe. But in the nineteenth century it was challenged. Paternalism, poverty relief and various other devices, it was said, had gone too far. At a time of enormous opportunity for economic expansion, when the markets of the world were at Britain's feet, it was said that English industry and trade, English labour were being inhibited by social restraints. So emerged the doctrines and the practices of *laissez faire*, or free enterprise, which for a time helped bring Britain to the peak of influence and power. But to some the price seemed too high. The slums of Manchester and London, the poverty, the sickness, the despair: these too seemed to be the consequence of *laissez faire*; and in despair there was alienation, violence, division, the ultimate prospect of the collapse of the unity of England. I believe, though there is no time to discuss it here, that the rediscovery of social responsibility in the late nineteenth century, merging into the welfare state of the twentieth, saved England from disaster. For they restored in a more sophisticated form the ideas about welfare and social responsibility—of *noblesse oblige*—which Shakespeare could have heard from some of the forward-looking members of parliament and pamphleteers in the London of Queen Elizabeth. Here was the doctrine that without social responsibility there is no security and stability, and when there is no security and stability liberty walks in danger.

I have argued in this paper that there were few men in Shakespeare's England who valued liberty above all things but that those few who did had set its value so high that they were prepared to sacrifice life itself to preserve it. 'Sweet indeed is the name of liberty,' said Peter Wentworth, 'and the thing itself a value beyond all inestimable treasure.'[1] Many of his fellow-countrymen set less store by liberty, but were involved increasingly in the tasks of social responsibility, whether they liked it or not. So in stability freedom could grow. I have argued, also, that since Puritanism was defeated in England but triumphed in America, the doctrine of equality has exercised less influence in our history than in that

[1] J. E. Neale, *Elizabeth I and her Parliaments, 1559–81* (1953), p. 319.

of the United States. We were forced therefore to search for an alternative doctrine and found it in an increasing measure of social commitment. The British welfare state was not invented by an English prime minister in 1945 but in the sixteenth century by the Elizabethans. We came—however reluctantly—to believe that by giving up some of our economic and social liberty we would preserve stability and create conditions for freedom to flourish. But we have had to learn this lesson over and over again in a constantly changing world. Thus, the paradox of liberty implicit in Shakespeare's England has become explicit to our own troubled generation who, seeing freedom in danger, may yet, in remembering its past, preserve its future.

VI

Visual and Rhetorical Imagery in Shakespeare's Plays[1]

DIETER MEHL

WHEN, under the impact of the actor's brilliant demonstration, the fascinating Pyrrhus-speech, Hamlet tries to imagine how this player would perform if he had to find adequate dramatic expression for an experience as disturbing as Hamlet's own, he draws a vigorous picture of an ideal theatrical performance:

> What would he do,
> Had he the motive and the cue for passion
> That I have? He would drown the stage with tears,
> And cleave the general ear with horrid speech;
> Make mad the guilty, and appal the free,
> Confound the ignorant, and amaze indeed
> The very faculties of eyes and ears. (II. ii. 553-9)

Most spectators will probably feel at this point that Hamlet is not only describing his own hopeful expectation of the *Mousetrap's* effect on the most prominent member of its audience, but that he is also expressing something very important about the very nature of Shakespearean drama: 'amaze indeed the very faculties of eyes and ears'. It is this dual appeal, the mutual illumination of visual and verbal effects, which would, I feel, repay closer investigation.

[1] A revised and slightly condensed version of a lecture given in German at the annual meeting of the Deutsche Shakespeare-Gesellschaft in Bochum in 1969, and published in *Jahrbuch der deutschen Shakespeare-Gesellschaft West*, 1970.
I wish to record my indebtedness to two valuable articles which only came to my attention after the substance of this study had been written: Robert Fricker, 'Das szenische Bild bei Shakespeare', *Annales Universitatis Saraviensis, Philosophie*, V (1956), 227-240, and Inga-Stina Ewbank, 'More Pregnantly than Words', *Shakespeare Survey*, 24 (1971), 13-18.

Here I can only suggest some lines of approach and draw attention to some previous studies which have not perhaps had the attention they deserve.

Hamlet is a very good example of the variety of dramatic devices employed by Shakespeare within a single play. It is aptly described by M. C. Bradbrook as 'a geological deposit of accumulated dramatic experience'.[1] A great deal of what has been written about it, in particular about the character of the hero, seems a little bookish because the play is so often seen primarily as a superb specimen of dramatic poetry, appealing to the intellect chiefly by means of highly sophisticated language. But *Hamlet* provides at the same time a most colourful dramatic spectacle; its visual appeal in any production that is not too spartan is very considerable and forms an indispensable part of our total conception of the play. Side by side with highly formalized rhetoric, such as the player's speech, there are pointed visual effects like the spectacle of old Hamlet's ghost (which, I believe, we should imagine as something rather more sensational than the average performance gives us), the resolutely warlike appearances of Fortinbras, presenting even visually a very sharp contrast to Hamlet's own mood, and the duel of the two young men who both are determined to avenge their fathers, a scene which could hardly fail to affect us as an image of distressing human waste. Apart from these obvious stage effects, there are a number of visual images expressing something beyond the power of the spoken word, allowing the eye to perceive some truth which the poetic language alone cannot convey.

The most striking example is the much-discussed dumb show preceding the players' performance. One of its dramatic functions, perhaps the most important, is to present in unmistakable gestures, without verbal explanation, the stark act of poisoning which so far has only been suggested through the medium of dramatic speech. This acts as a very forceful reminder of the events preceding the first scene of the play, and it also demonstrates the theatre's power to speak to us through both language and gesture.

The graveyard scene is perhaps even more important for our understanding of the play's action. The witty dialogue between

[1] *Shakespeare the Craftsman* (London, 1969), p. 122.

Hamlet and the grave-digger in which Hamlet shows a composure and readiness for death which we have not seen in him before is commented on by the visual presence of the skull. Hamlet finds himself confronted, in a very concrete manner, with the reality of death that has occupied his thoughts throughout the play. At the beginning, his father's ghost had opened his eyes to a new and very disquieting aspect of death. The idea of his own end had then led him to a meditation about the nature of death in general. Now the scene in which the grave-digger's spade begins to unearth the bones of men long deceased turns into a visual *memento mori* by means of which the question of death is illuminated from yet another angle, the passing of time. Hamlet experiences death in a new form, one that illustrates its universal independence of place and time, thus transcending all his earlier reflections. Confronted with the image of the skull, his desire for revenge seems to lose some of its relevance and urgency, and a new stage of the play begins which might be characterized by Hamlet's own words, 'the readiness is all'. It is hardly possible to think of another dramatic device that could achieve this expansion of the play's ideas into universal significance in such a precise and impressive manner.

In the second part of the same scene the dependence of the play's events on the omnipotence of death is again revealed through the visual impact of the action. Laertes, embracing the corpse of his sister within her grave, does not only present an unconscious anticipation of his own death—he even points to this wider significance of the action by asking the grave-digger to 'pile your dust upon the quick and dead'. The words have an almost liturgical ring, bringing out the full meaning of the dramatic spectacle. Finally, it will be obvious to every reader, and even more to the spectator, that the subsequent struggle between Hamlet and Laertes over (or perhaps even within) Ophelia's grave has again a symbolic and clearly prophetic effect.

I have dwelt on *Hamlet* because in this play, which is so often discussed purely in literary terms, there is such a rich variety of dramatic devices that it makes a particularly good example of the various techniques employed by Shakespeare to combine verbal and visual effects.

When I use the terms 'visual effects' or 'stage image' I am not merely referring to actual gestures or stage directions implied in the dialogue, but to all those elements in the plays that appeal to the visual sense and thereby carry some part of the play's meaning simultaneously with or even beyond the words spoken by the characters. My remarks on *Hamlet* have already shown that the action on the stage is not merely designed to illustrate what is spoken, but that it can, by implication, often go beyond what is explicitly stated in the text. This aspect of Shakespeare's art has been comparatively little examined, although a few valuable recent studies show that it has not escaped notice. It is still fair to say, however, that the average reader thinks of Shakespeare mainly as a literary experience, and though there are good reasons for this and it would be foolish to go to the opposite extreme, it seems to me that often a very important dimension of his text is missed.

The Elizabethan playwrights, and Shakespeare in particular, were remarkably successful in utilizing for their own purposes two very distinct lines of tradition: classical rhetoric and what might loosely be described as popular spectacle or pageantry in its widest sense. Early Elizabethan plays are often surprising in their seemingly arbitrary juxtaposition of very heterogeneous forms of representation. Side by side with lavishly-designed and quickly-moving dumb shows or improvised, hardly articulated knock-about farce, we find scenes of highly formalized dialogue or stately speeches, heavily cluttered with rhetorical embellishment, losing all touch with the actual stage. The visual part of drama often seems like a piece of entertainment and diversion for the benefit of those who are unable to derive much edification from the literary qualities of the play. This can be said also of some of the earlier moralities, and especially of the civic pageants and allegorical shows devised by various communities for religious or political festivals. In many cases we may even assume that the physical conditions of the performance made it virtually impossible for many spectators to understand what was being said. The visual effect therefore had to be sufficiently obvious and entertaining for everybody to have some fun and to draw some moral. An interesting example is provided by one of Thomas Heywood's shows. The stage-direction runs as follows:

> The third Pageant or Show meerly consisteth of Anticke gesticulations, dances, and other Mimicke postures, devised onely for the vulgar, who are better delighted with that which pleaseth the eye, than contenteth the eare.[1]

Many Elizabethan plays are obviously designed to appeal to the tastes of such spectators as well as of the more sophisticated listeners, as could be illustrated from numerous stage directions. This is, however, only one aspect of Shakespeare's visual dramaturgy, and it is, perhaps, the less important one. More significant is the fact that for many Elizabethans an image was capable in a particularly effective and meaningful way, of conveying pregnant ideas and moral truths without the aid of words. This is not only true with regard to the vulgar crowd, unable to grasp subtle meanings, but it applies, according to widely accepted Renaissance theories, also on a much higher level. The often-documented and to us strangely unfamiliar Elizabethan interest in all kinds of allegorical representations, collections of emblems, heraldic devices, hieroglyphics, and significant if not easily decipherable graphic or plastic compositions can only be explained by their belief that through the eyes we can perceive the essence of things which the intrinsically limited and often clumsy tools of the language cannot express. Pushed to its logical conclusion, this idea leads to the theory, held by Neoplatonists, that the human eye alone, by-passing our rational faculties, is capable of true perception. In practice this would mean that by looking at an allegorical tableau a spectator could learn something about the nature of whatever is represented (usually some moral or political commonplace) which could not be expressed by words alone. Historians of the visual arts have known for a long time how immensely significant such theories are for any adequate understanding of Renaissance art, and there have been valuable attempts

---

[1] *Londini Speculum*, 1637, quoted from R. H. Shepherd's edition (London, 1874), vol. IV.

G

to apply these insights to the study of Renaissance theatre which is based, at least in part, on very similar ways of thinking. It is generally known, for instance, that Ben Jonson's masques can only be fully appreciated with reference to iconographic traditions. They appeal to the visual perception of the spectator in a way closely resembling the method of some Renaissance painters. Thus, Botticelli, depicting the Birth of Venus in a way that strongly suggests iconographic conventions of Christ's baptism, or representing *Primavera* as a kind of visual analogy to the Annunciation, succeeds in creating complex impressions that can be but insufficiently elucidated by verbal interpretation.[1]

Similar effects can be traced in the plays of Shakespeare. The famous moment of Perdita's discovery by the old Shepherd in *The Winter's Tale* has been seen by many critics as a visual symbol of one of the play's main themes, expressed concisely in the words: 'Now bless thyself; thou met'st with things dying, I with things new-born.' Moelwyn Merchant has drawn attention to the fact that later illustrators of Shakespeare repeatedly selected this scene and drew it in a way that is strongly reminiscent of the birth of Christ, as a kind of secularized nativity scene.[2] It would of course be rash to make such an observation the basis of a Christian reading of the play, and we cannot be sure whether in this case we are not dealing with a later over-interpretation of some far less significant event in the play. There are, however, in Shakespeare's plays, other scenes where the image presented on the stage suggests a deeper significance without its necessarily being put into explicit words. This can be achieved in very different ways, as the introductory remarks on *Hamlet* tried to point out, and it can hardly be denied that the Elizabethan dramatists had more than just rhetorical language at their command when it came to expressing complex meanings.

Often spectacle can function as a kind of visual metaphor to give wider significance to the action by stylizing the individual event

---

[1] I owe some of these examples to Muriel C. Bradbrook's most stimulating study, *Shakespeare and Elizabethan Poetry* (London, 1951).

[2] In an unpublished lecture given in 1956. See also his *Shakespeare and the Artist* (London, 1959), pp. 208 ff. and plates 39a and 77b.

into a timeless human situation. Brutus' suicide is a simple example: the picture of a Roman throwing himself on to his sword is used in some of the best-known emblem books as an illustration of the sentence: *Fortuna virtutem superans*. Without going into the question, not immediately relevant anyway, whether Shakespeare was directly influenced by these emblem books, it can safely be assumed that the corresponding scene in *Julius Caesar* would suggest certain associations to the better-read Elizabethan play-goer beyond the mere words of the dialogue. Apart from this scene, it is interesting to see in what way death as a visual symbol dominates large stretches of the play. This is particularly obvious in the last part and in those scenes where the corpse of Caesar governs the action by its mere presence, as Maurice Charney has shown.[1] The dead body of Caesar is particularly effective as a piece of symbolic spectacle, illustrating the violation of the order of the commonwealth, and it is addressed as such by Antony. His brilliant rhetoric not only appeals to the intellect of his listeners, as Brutus largely does, but, just like the theatre itself, it succeeds in taking advantage of visual effects as well. While Brutus tries to present the murder of Caesar as a sacrificial act, as an almost sacred rite which must not be described as 'a savage spectacle', it is just this gruesome and horrifying aspect of death which is emphasized by Antony. His own interpretation of the facts is effectively supported by the description of the visual details. Following the principle of rhetorical climax, he starts by presenting Caesar's blood-soaked robe which he addresses as a symbol of his dead friend. The sight of the torn and stained garment is meant to open the eyes of the spectators to the true nature of the butchery, and only when the symbolic object has achieved its full effect does Antony reveal the body itself. This spectacle now makes all further rhetoric unnecessary, or rather it is

---

[1] *Shakespeare's Roman Plays* (Cambridge, Mass., 1961), p. 52; some of my examples are also used, with different emphasis, by Martha H. Golden, in her stimulating paper, 'Stage Imagery in Shakespearean Studies', *Shakespearean Research Opportunities*, 1 (1965), 10–20; many more examples, not all of them relevant to my own argument, are given in her unpublished dissertation, *The Iconography of the English History Play* (Columbia, 1964), a very interesting study full of valuable material.

an integral part of his rhetoric, combining verbal skill with visual
effect employed just at the appropriate moment:

> Kind souls, what weep you when you but behold
> Our Caesar's vesture wounded? Look you here,
> Here is himself, marr'd as you see with traitors.
> *First Cit.* O piteous spectacle! . . . O most bloody sight!
> (III. ii. 195–202)

It is important to note that this scene (which Shakespeare did not
find in Plutarch) is not directly addressed to the audience in the
theatre, but the audience witnesses an act of dramatic persuasion,
watching its effect on the Roman mob. It is obvious, however,
that the whole play works in a very similar manner, and its
rhetoric includes visual effects just like Antony's. There is little
doubt that the Elizabethan spectator was much better trained at
recognizing and appreciating such effects because of a long familiarity with iconographic conventions and allegorical shows.

Another aspect of this technique which has been brought to our
notice chiefly by such historians of the visual arts as E. Panowski,
E. Gombrich, and S. Chew is the use of symbolic properties in the
plays of Shakespeare and his contemporaries. It is possible that this
aspect has sometimes been overestimated, but it is still important
to bear in mind that for the Elizabethans many objects had their
firmly established traditional connotations which made them particularly suitable as symbols, emphasizing certain aspects of the
plays' action. A close examination of Shakespeare's use of stage
properties would probably indicate that he often exploits the ico-
nographical associations of objects, like Shylock's pair of scales,
Falstaff's by now notorious cushion, Macbeth's dagger, or Cleo-
patra's vipers. A more complex case is provided by the clothes
metaphor which appears so frequently in Shakespeare and his contemporaries. The putting on or taking off of clothes, one's own or
somebody else's, fitting or assumed and pretending, is time and
again associated with the acts of disguise, deceit, pretence, or
genuine transformation of character. Garments are the reflection
of the whole personality, as in the case of dead Caesar, and this can

be brought out by means of stage action as well as through metaphorical language.

This close association between garments and particular states of mind is, it has often been noticed, a particularly important feature in *Macbeth*. Very near the beginning we are told of Macbeth:

> New honours come upon him,
> Like our strange garments, cleave not to their mould
> But with the aid of use. (I. iv. 144–6)

The events on the stage are a concrete manifestation of this metaphor. The couple's rise to royal dignity is apparent in their robes and the strange and therefore ill-fitting garments are the outward sign of an inner discrepancy between Macbeth and his assumed state. Granville-Barker described the brief scene between Macbeth and his wife immediately before the banquet very fittingly: 'The royal robes, stiff on their bodies—stiff as with caked blood—seem to keep them apart.'[1] Of course, this again is only a metaphorical commentary, but it suggests very accurately the way in which the action on the stage informs us about the inner state of the murderers. In other ways, too, the play provides expressive stage images accompanying and adding emphasis to the dramatic action, such as the appearance of the witches, the banquet broken up by the ghost of Banquo, and the pantomimic prophecy showing Banquo's descendants as Macbeth's heirs, illustrating more clearly than anything else in the play Macbeth's final delusion and his short-lived triumph. In the course of the play he himself more and more turns into an embodiment of tyranny. Macduff hints at this depersonalized aspect of the action when in the final battle he addresses his adversary:

> Then yield thee, coward,
> And live to be the show and gaze o'th' time.
> We'll have thee, as our rarer monsters are,
> Painted upon a pole, and underwrit
> 'Here may you see the tyrant.' (v. viii. 23–7)

[1] Quoted by Kenneth Muir in his Arden Edition of the play, p. 84.

In some respect this is far more than a boastful threat because the whole play has already made it very real: 'Here may you see the tyrant.' The idea is, however, explicitly taken up again in the last scene when Macduff brings in the tyrant's head, presumably on a pole, and presents it to the new king:

> Behold, where stands
> Th' usurper's cursed head. The time is free.
> I see thee compass'd with thy kingdom's pearl.
>   (v. viii. 45–6)

Very often Shakespeare's characters point at themselves or at others in this way and this usually means that the scene is given a more general application beyond the immediate situation. A very different example is the wrongly accused Queen Hermione, presenting herself as an image of suffering innocence. The whole scene thus becomes a tableau of an unjust tribunal. It can generally be said that state and court scenes by their ritual character lend themselves well to a more emblematic way of staging and often seem to be conceived in that way. It is not surprising that the most comprehensive full-scale study of stage-imagery should be devoted to the histories, where nearly every scene turns into a symbolic picture of the state of the commonwealth, the blessings or the dangers of kingship, or the periodic alternation of discord, rebellion, national unity, war, and peace.

It would be impossible within this limited space, and could in any case only lead to a superficial listing of examples, to examine every play of Shakespeare's from the point of view of their visual effects, but it is interesting to consider Shakespeare's use of this dramatic device at various stages of his artistic career because there seem to be very clear variations which are important for our understanding of the plays.

In his earliest plays there is often an obvious, even literal correspondence between verbal and scenic images, between rhetoric and dramatic action. The plays were misunderstood and consequently depreciated as long as the action on the stage was taken as the immediate representation of actual events. In fact, however, as recent criticism has made clear, it seems that Shakespeare, especially in *Titus Andronicus*, was trying to achieve something very similar to his narrative poems; he creates a series of changing tableaux which are explained by the rhetorical imagery of the accompanying speeches. There is a very close correspondence here between visual and verbal rhetoric, both equally far removed from any modern conception of realism. The spectacle of the ravished Lavinia, her hands and tongue cut off, present on the stage through several scenes, is not just gruesome realism or sensational theatre of cruelty; rather it is a daring attempt at visualizing a pregnant metaphor. Repeatedly Lavinia is described by spectators on the stage; she is compared to a tree with its branches lopped off, and to Procne who in Ovid's *Metamorphoses* meets a similar fate. Lavinia thus becomes a visual symbol of ravished nature, one of the main themes of the play, and at the same time a kind of reincarnation of a classical myth that is several times referred to in the course of the play. We may justly ask whether Shakespeare's experiment with this kind of poetic drama was really successful, but it is important to recognize the precise quality of this experiment and to realize that he has perhaps only carried to an extreme a principle of dramatic representation that is characteristic of Elizabethan drama and one which he never abandoned completely.

The literal manner in which metaphorical expressions and images are translated into concrete dramatic action has a distinctly artificial quality, but it seems to be in keeping with the general dramaturgy of the Elizabethan theatre and to depend on an audience capable of appreciating symbolic connotations in the tableau on the stage. This is apparent from the first scene of the play in which the struggle for power in Rome and for Lavinia is expressed in such unmistakable, even statuesque stage action that the gist of the story could almost be grasped by a spectator without help from the dialogue. The same technique is applied to some of the localities, like the barren landscape in which Lavinia is raped, and to persons, like the Moor Aaron whose character, he tells us, is of the same hue as his face. His tête-à-tête with Tamora in the woods seems to have its literal effect on her; her honour becomes as dark as the colour of his skin, and, to complete the image, she gives birth to a black baby which is displayed on the stage and addressed as a visual symbol of this sinister alliance. Titus bewails his fate before a heap of stones which serves as an emblem of the fruitlessness of his complaints, and in his madness he shoots arrows at the sun with messages for the gods above, imploring them for just revenge; finally he has his hand chopped off to rescue his sons. All these events speak for themselves in an over-explicit, literal way, and almost any single scene could be used to demonstrate that all the seemingly naturalistic presentation of the action only serves as a vehicle for a clear elucidation of inner developments and moral truths, a dramatic technique that has been very suitably described by Muriel Bradbrook as 'moral heraldry'.

Just how well this term applies to early Shakespearean drama can be illustrated by the famous Temple-Garden scene in *1 Henry VI* where heraldic devices, the white and red roses, are actually brought on to the stage as graphic symbols of the two factions. The highly stylized stage action, accompanied by elaborate rhetoric, is an almost obtrusively obvious presentation of the outbreak of the War of the Roses. Once more, verbal images and spectacle are related in a literal manner. In this case, as in some others mentioned, the visual symbolism is also apparent to the reader, but its full impact can only be achieved in performance.

This striking dramatic technique is not confined to Shakespeare's early plays, though it is used more sparingly and less obviously in his later tragedies. The putting out of Gloucester's eyes in *King Lear* is the most impressive example. Here again, as many commentators have noticed, an internal event has been translated into a very telling stage action, producing a visual metaphor of a very suggestive quality. The blinding of Gloucester is an apt symbol of his inability to face the truth about himself and his family. At the same time we have the almost paradoxical fact that Gloucester does not learn true perception until he has lost his eyesight, just as Lear himself only becomes a true king when all his traditional regalia have been stripped off. The words of the play again and again emphasize this literal though complex correspondence between outward and inward events.

But for all the similarity with the early plays, there is here a new element and Shakespeare clearly goes beyond his earlier technique. The visual part of the action is not just a decorative extension of the poetic language, and there is hardly the same duplication of verbal and visual effects; rather they supplement and enrich each other in such a way that the visual impression adds to the meaning of the words and *vice versa*.

When in the first scene of the play, Lear, with a map of his kingdom in front of him, divides his realm and shortly afterwards, pointing at Cordelia, describes her just as he had previously described the various parts of his land, it becomes clear even through the grouping of the characters on stage that for him she is now only an object like the dowries he has shared out. This is emphasized by his choice of words:

> Sir, there she stands:
> If aught within that little seeming substance,
> Or all of it, with our displeasure piec'd,
> And nothing more, may fitly like your Grace,
> She's there, and she is yours. (I. i. 197–201)

His parting from Cordelia, which he proclaims and puts into practice by his decisive gesture, is the beginning of his sufferings. The two do not meet again until the fourth act, and here again the visual element is almost more important than the words. Cordelia is accompanied by her supporters, whereas Lear confronts her on his own in almost the same helpless and humble attitude as hers in the first scene. Between these two moments are all those scenes in which Lear has to learn wisdom from the fool by becoming a fool himself and by recognizing his own folly. The inner process is continually underlined by the action on the stage, as in the scene where the fool offers his cap first to Lear and then to Kent, or at the end of the fourth scene when Lear leaves Goneril in a rage, the fool running after him: 'Nuncle Lear, nuncle Lear, tarry—take the fool with thee.' It is interesting to see how the actual events are anticipated by such images as well as by verbal metaphors. As early as the fifth scene the fool tells Lear that he has lost his wits and Lear himself speaks of this possibility: 'O, let me not be mad, not mad, sweet heaven!' His fears will soon become literally true.

Just as the fool more and more acts as a visual symbol of Lear's own state of mind, the naked Edgar, reduced to mere animality, is seen by Lear as an image of himself: 'Didst thou give all to thy daughters? And art thou come to this?' This is particularly important in the moving scene where Lear is tearing off his clothes in order to become like Edgar: 'Unaccommodated man is no more but such a poor, bare, forked animal as thou art. Off, off, you lendings!' Again the stage action expresses something which could hardly be put into words, the complete degradation of the king and a return to the bare essentials of human existence. It is, at the same time, a very literal use of the clothes metaphor. In spite of this, however, the action does not lose in dramatic reality, and this seems to me a very important difference between *King Lear* and *Titus Andronicus*. Although Edgar and Lear at times assume the character of depersonalized emblems, they still remain individual dramatic personalities in a sense Aaron and Lavinia are not. There is, in *King Lear*, an organic blending of symbolic spectacle and dramatic stage action and this is, in varying degrees, true of all the major tragedies. Again and again the verbal expression is enriched by visual metaphor, but this interplay of action and language is so unobtrusive that it is easily overlooked. Gloucester is, of course, a very real and individually drawn character, and yet at the same time he is made to appear to the spectator as a personification of human blindness. Similarly, Lear's own career could not be adequately described in general terms, but there are undoubtedly some very typical elements in his gradual progress from the pompous display of royal splendour in the first scene to naked helplessness, madness, and wisdom at the point of death. An abstraction like this is bound to sound oversimplified, but perhaps it can suggest something that is present in the play and is conveyed to the spectator mainly through the visible action on the stage.

It would, however, be unwise to generalize unguardedly about the emblematic nature of gestures, scenes and properties or to take for granted on the part of the Elizabethan audiences an easy familiarity with all the iconographic conventions collected by modern scholarship. It is, moreover, particularly important not to lose sight of the development of the Elizabethan stage during the period under consideration. The evidence of the plays suggests that this development is complicated by the interaction of partially opposed trends. There is, on the one hand, a growing tendency towards a more realistic presentation of life on the stage, a tendency that appears much earlier in the theatres on the continent and that explains some of the obvious differences between *Titus Andronicus* and *King Lear*.

We often find, on the other hand, a striking return to some older methods of presentation in the emergence of the masque and in the revived interest in all kinds of allegorical spectacle, and this in turn seems to have become more and more dominant. In many of these visual entertainments there are no rhetorical speeches in the traditional sense, and we find a very sparing use of poetic imagery and metaphor. The expository speech of Time between the two halves of *The Winter's Tale* is a good example of this new unadorned simplicity of dramatic language. It is completely different from the passionate bravura of the Chorus in *Henry V*, and this may illustrate a new emphasis on the non-verbal elements in the later plays. It has often been noticed that in the romances something of the powerful concentration and intensity in the poetry of the great tragedies has disappeared. The style often seems strangely muted and relaxed in comparison with the violence and energy of the action and the emotions. The speeches do not, on the whole, attempt to suggest subtle nuances of thought and atmosphere or to point towards a universal application by means of complex images, but there is far more reliance on the suggestive quality of the action itself. This can be seen very clearly in *The Winter's Tale*, as, for instance, in Leontes' sudden jealousy, which, whatever may be its dramatic function, is only very superficially prepared and motivated in the text of the play. Similarly, in the sheep-shearing scene, the stage action seems often more impressive than the dialogue; even when a rational discussion develops, as in the brief argument about art and nature between Perdita and Polixenes, it is inseparable from the visual accompaniment.

The most impressive example of the predominance of the visual over dialogue is the reappearance of Hermione as staged by Paulina. Glynne Wickham has convincingly demonstrated that the statue of Hermione presented to Leontes should not be pictured like one of those pleasant figures we find in eighteenth-century parks, but as an effigy of the kinds to be seen in many churches and chapels.[1] What we witness in the play, then, is not just the coming to life of a work of art, but the resurrection of the dead, the literal overcoming of the grave by the power of life. Again the visual action here conveys something that is hardly present in the dialogue, at least not in the same explicit and at the same time symbolic manner.

In *The Tempest* the relation between language and spectacle is even more strange. Here again a very important part of the action is presented in the form of memorable images, illustrating, almost in the manner of *tableaux vivants*, certain stages in the action: the sleeping Miranda as an image of innocence, the appearance of Ferdinand as the embodiment of a world as yet unknown to her, Caliban as an emblem of bestial, uncivilized nature, and, finally, the pantomime produced by Prospero which again is a visual treatment of some of the play's main themes by means of symbol and visual metaphor. The way in which figures of speech and verbal concepts are translated into stage action could almost be described as a return to the style of the early plays. Again the clothes metaphor is frequently employed: when we hear Gonzalo meditating about his clothes having been freshly washed in the shipwreck, his argument is obviously underlined or even ironically questioned by the actual image on the stage; there is a very similar effect later in the same scene when Antonio points at himself to prove how well he plays his part—a part that he will have to abandon very soon:

> And look how well my garments sit upon me;
> Much feater than before. (II.i.263-4)

---

[1] *Shakespeare's Dramatic Heritage* (London, 1969), pp. 263-5.

The most literal staging of the same metaphor occurs when Ariel successfully misleads Caliban, Stephano and Trinculo by producing splendid but immaterial garments for them whose unreal nature is a pregnant symbol of Caliban's unfounded hopes and expectations. The translation of the clothes metaphor into dramatic action is much more direct here than in *Macbeth*. By this kind of visual stylization the action of the play almost becomes a parable, and this quality clearly relates *The Tempest* to the court masque.

Another metaphor, the relation of the world to a stage, is acted out in a more literal manner here than in the earlier plays. Prospero's art not only creates illusion and meaningful spectacle, it often turns the characters themselves into actors, paralysing their own free will. He separates and unites people, he displays them to others like an impresario to achieve particular effects, as in his 'discovering' of Ferdinand and Miranda at their game of chess as a tableau of innocence and love. These statuesque scenes provide a good illustration of the change in Shakespeare's methods of dramatic presentation, his increasing reliance on scenic effects, and a corresponding reduction of verbal complexity and virtuosity. The dialogue often has the simplicity of the masques and it has been claimed with regard to this play that a silent production would be able to convey more of the total meaning than would be possible in any other Shakespearean play. This does not mean that *The Tempest* is lacking in dramatic poetry; the contrary is true, but the dialogue and the longer speeches often seem strangely unrelated to the spectacle on the stage. There is far less of that intricate interplay of word and gesture which is so characteristic of the great tragedies. The stage action is neither a literal extension of elaborate rhetoric by visual means, as in *Titus Andronicus*, nor does it arise organically from the poetry, as in the great tragedies, but seems almost independent of it and contributes as much to the total meaning of the play as the language. A purely literary interpretation which disregards the visual appeal of these plays is thus particularly inadequate in the case of Shakespeare's late romances.

This leads to the truism that Shakespeare's plays only reveal their full meaning in performance, but it also raises the question of how the visual elements of the plays would have been brought out in an Elizabethan production. It is a problem that has not received sufficient attention, mainly perhaps because there has often been a certain lack of communication between historians of the Elizabethan theatre and literary critics. If it is true, however, that visual symbolism in varying forms and degrees is an important part of Shakespeare's dramatic style, then we shall have to use our knowledge of Shakespeare's theatre more effectively to test and to supplement literary interpretations. This could not only lead to a fuller and more adequate understanding of Elizabethan drama, but it could also be of help in our search for a meaningful contemporary form of Shakespearean production.

VII

A Study in Retirement, 1660–1700

SYBIL ROSENFELD

Of all periods the Restoration must be the most difficult to sum up neatly into a phrase; in all its self-contradictory variety it defies the epigram. Think of it as irreligious and you will be confronted by a spate of books on divinity and a series of notable divines; think of it as frivolous and the founders and members of the Royal Society will confound your generalizations. Men indeed had seen such sudden and complete reversals of old and new orders that they were apt to distrust the stability of all things in heaven and on earth. They were in experimental mood, intensely curious about life, ready to try living in a variety of ways. We think of the ways as urban and highly social and of this age as one that had no use for solitude, that mocked at retirement from the London world, that heaped with ridicule the coarse country gentleman and his out-of-fashion family. Indeed, to be away from the glitter of the court circle was for most men to be in exile. Thus Congreve found the only pleasures in Tunbridge were in letters from his friends:

> When you suppose the Country agreeable to me [he wrote to one of them] you suppose such Reasons why it should be so, that while I read your Letter I am of your Mind; but when I look off, I find I am only charm'd with the Landskip which you have drawn. So that if I would see a fine Prospect of the Country I must desire you to send it me from the Town.

Etherege too, when he heard that the Duke of Buckingham had voluntarily retired to his Yorkshire estate, was horror-stricken. It was as incredible to him as the news of the French King's turning Benedictine monk or the Pope's setting up for a beau. How could a man accustomed to the airs and graces of the court be content, he remonstrated, with the society of a country parson or an 'heiress apparent of a thatch'd Cottage, in a straw Hat' and 'the nonsensical Chat and barbarous Languages of Farmers'. These are but two voices among a multitude, for it was the general tenor of men's thought that 'the sedate, contemplative life' was dull, and dullness a sin against society. The comedies are forever gibing at country life and in them the ill-mannered, unsophisticated squire is a never-failing figure of fun. But life in the Restoration was not only what the comedies, written to please a court audience, made of it, and we are all too inclined to acquire from them a one-sided view. In this matter of the country we are apt to neglect that little group of serious men who found in it the only ultimate satisfaction.

They had their exemplars. Had not Cowley, a major poet and a greater than Milton in their eyes, spent his last years in long-wished-for solitude? And Marvell, though a lesser influence, had sung his gardens and green shades. Besides, the troublous times of the Commonwealth had sent families to places safer than London was, so that many young men of King Charles II's reign had been bred in country ways. Evelyn spent his early years among the gardens of Wotton and Sayes Court, George Savile (later Marquess of Halifax) married young and settled at Rufford, and even the Cromwellian Temples lived on their estate in Ireland.

At the Restoration Halifax and Temple entered the whirl of politics, accepted diplomatic posts, carried out intricate negotiations, and wearied in the end of the fret and fever of Whitehall. Little wonder in such a time of political uncertainty when no one knew for which king the bells of London would next peal. Not uncertainty only, but intrigue, plots, secret cabals; a life in which there could be no sincerity and no peace:

A wasps' nest [Halifax found] is a quieter place to sleep in than this town to live in which maketh me so weary of it that you must not wonder if you hear that, notwithstanding my passion for London, . . . I go very early this spring in the country.

Temple consistently refused high offices of state, thereby earn-
ing the censure of Macaulay; but it was not only a pusillanimous
refusal to shoulder responsibility in dangerous moments, it was
also a disgust with the political game and a conviction that the
ultimate meaning of his life would be found in his orchard and his
library. He was but half-heartedly a statesman, since he was by
nature a country gentleman. Even when he was leading an entertaining, easy life as ambassador in Brussels, he wrote to Lord Lisle:
'My Imaginations run very often over the Pleasures of the Air and
the Earth, and the Water, but much more of the conversation at
Sheen.' To his gardens at Sheen he more than once retired, and
was more than once tempted forth again, until in 1680 he finally
took his leave of public life after twenty years' experience 'of the
uncertainty of princes—the caprices of fortune—the corruption of
ministers—the violence of factions—the unsteadiness of counsels,
and the infidelity of friends'. He looked down the vista of his
years forever abjuring all 'those airy visions which have so long
busied my head about mending the world and at the same time of
all those shining toys or follies that employ the thought of busy
men'. Temple's significance was not, as Macaulay would have us
believe, in his career, but in that very pottering in the orchard
that he condemns. To posterity the 'Essay on the Gardens of
Epicurus' is made of more enduring stuff than the abortive Triple
Alliance. Temple himself had a true sense of values; country
life, he said, was the inclination of his youth and the pleasure of
his age;

> and I can truly say, that among many great employments that
> have fallen to my share, I have never asked or sought for any
> one of them, but often endeavoured to escape from them, into
> the ease and freedom of a private scene, where a man may go his
> own way and his own pace in the common paths or circles of
> life.

For him it was the fuller and the better life, and when he came
to die he requested that his heart might be laid near the sundial in
the sweet retreat of his garden.

H

How did the Temples and the Evelyns pass their days in the retirement they so loved? In books and in conversation and in writings, above all in the precious care of their gardens. As in every sphere, so in horticulture there were new experiments. Science was being applied to the growing of trees and production of fruit. Temple considered that flowers were a woman's business and concentrated loving care on his orchards until he could justly be proud of his plums and boast that his orange trees were as large as almost any he saw in France.

Landscape gardening, 'this later and universal luxury of the whole nation', as Evelyn called it, was coming into its own and the way was preparing for Capability Brown and the fashioning of some of the great estates of England. The interest centred in Evelyn, who had seen the best gardens of Italy and France and was always ready to lend an eager ear to news of a new ingenious device for grotto, fountain, or sundial.

The ideal was Horatian: good friends, good books, leisure and content. There is a description by an anonymous letter-writer of a perfect country day which would have pleased the Roman:

> I rise every Morning at Five or earlier, Study till Nine, then take my Morning's Draught, return to my Study till Noon; After Dinner a Pipe and a Cup of true brew'd English Ale, an hour or two of Conversation, and then with a Book we take a Walk in the most delicious Promenade in the World, either on a woody Hill, with a gentle, murmuring Rivulet beneath; or else on the Brink of that, through a winding Valley, with verdant and easie Hill on both sides, cloathed with Trees and pleasant Meadows in the Intervals. There Horace, Vergil, Milton, Dryden or some such Heroes entertain us, till satisfied, not surfeited with Pleasure.

Other writers stress the moral and practical value, making a point of it that such a way of living was conducive to virtue and piety, even to physical well-being and longevity. Evelyn, for such reasons, praised the gardener's life, and Temple found that air, verdure and exercise improved 'both contemplation and health and enjoyment of sense and imaginations, and thereby the quiet

and ease both of the body and mind'. But there is delight too in
this life for its own sake without thought of improvement, as in
Algernon Sidney's feeling about his Tivoli villa: 'Nature, art and
treasure can hardly make a place more pleasant than this; the
description would look more like poetry than truth.'
Halifax put it down to 'the general disease of loving home', and
how sincere in truth is the note he strikes in a letter to his brother:

> I confess I dream of the country as men do of small beer when
> they are in a fever, and at this time poor Rufford with all its
> wrinkles hath more charms for me than anything London can
> shew me.

Whether or no one thinks these men had an authentic love of
nature depends on what one means by that phrase. In the romantic
manner they certainly had not. She was not for them the robe of
God; they did not find in her any manifestation of spirit, any pan-
theistic significance whatever. She is no inspiration to lyric flights,
and no word-magic is woven about her wonders. Yet the 'wood-
born' Evelyn loved trees, exclaiming in his *Diary* with spontane-
ous joy at the sight of 'goodly walks and hills shaded with yew
and box'. He loved them too to practical purpose, writing his
Sylva, or a Discourse of Forest Trees for their protection, and therein
waxing indignant with the forest-despoilers of Cromwell's day
for their destruction of so goodly a thing. Spiritual centuries
apart perhaps from Wordsworth, who was stirred to poetry by his
own boyish despoliation of the woods, realizing it was a violation
of the spirit; yet one cannot think that nature was altogether
without spiritual value to that little group of men who buried
themselves in green retreats. In a restless and uncertain age they
found in her tranquillity, security, and inward peace.

VIII

Biblical Translation in the Eighteenth Century[1]

SUSIE I. TUCKER

MY topic is eighteenth-century biblical translation. 'Meanly and imperfectly expressed.' That is not a recent comment from some literary critic writing about the New English Bible, but a remark from that influential eighteenth-century periodical, the *Critical Review*,[2] on the Authorized Version itself.

Dr. Wendeborn, a Lutheran pastor settled in London, gives it as his opinion that:

> The Translation of the Bible was formerly regarded as a standard, as a classic of the language, and Dr. Johnson in his Dictionary quoted it frequently as an authority; but it is at present no more so. Many words which occur in the Bible and the orthography of some would at present not be used by good writers. It has several times been proposed to make a New Translation for common use, and under authority, but, hitherto, it has been of no effect.[3]

However, there were plenty of scholars in the eighteenth century who tried to produce versions of the Bible more acceptable to the taste, knowledge, and usage of the time, though none of them attained any official standing, not even those of Archbishop New-combe. The reasons given to justify any sort of new version were various and valid. The deepening of scholarship, the changes in English usage, both semantic and syntactical, the growth of new associations with old words, are all mentioned. They happen in

[1] The sixth Arundell Esdaile Memorial Lecture, delivered 12 November 1970.
[2] 25, p. 108.
[3] *View of England* (1791), II, 39.

every age, and therefore no translation can ever be made into an English which is 'timeless'.

One translator, John Worsley of Hertford, published a New Testament 'according to the present idiom of the English Tongue'. This was in 1770, but he considered that the continual change of English necessitated a new revision by public authority at least once a century.

When the *Monthly Review*[1] had this version before it, it noted that:

> where the common version speaks of a *mote* in the eye, the word is now changed for *chaff* or *splinter*, instead of the awkward phrase, *we do you to wit, we make known to you*, and where *shall* is used for *will*, *should* for *would*, or the contrary they are altered.

These are minor alterations in keeping with more modern usage.

Ten years later, the same magazine[2] thought that Joseph Priestley's *Harmony of the Evangelists* was in general 'just and judicious'; it quotes his modernizations of some passages where the old wording could be misleading—e.g., 'Be not anxious' for 'Take no thought', 'Explain this parable' for 'Declare this parable', *livelihood* for *living*, *trade* for *occupy*. But Dr. Priestley should have altered 'lay a dying', which is 'a very inelegant expression'.

A problem that inevitably confronts every translator is how to render the idiom of one language in terms of another, especially when time, social conditions, and climate are as different as those of modern England and the periods and countries of the Scriptures.

Opinions differed. In 1736 the *Gentleman's Magazine*, with a new version of a psalm before it, remarked that poetry especially cannot be translated literally:

> Different nations have different ways of speaking: And a word or manner of expression which is both Familiar and Elegant in one, would be unintelligible or ridiculous by being literally translated into another.[3]

[1] XLIII (1771), 11.
[2] LXIV (1781), 87.
[3] VI (1736), 509.

Indeed, if Hebrew would go into English word for word, it would be a greater miracle than any recorded in the Bible!

On the other hand, in 1763 the *Monthly Review*[1] thought somewhat differently when it was dealing with a New Translation of the Psalms from the Hebrew Original by William Green. The *Review* thinks that:

> the Translator's great caution in avoiding Hebrew idioms is no advantage at all . . . since these Hebrew idioms, having been so long used in former translations, are become as familiar as English ones, and, in general, as well understood.

Mr. Spectator thought the same:

> It happens very luckily [he says, in his 405th paper] that the *Hebrew* idioms run into the *English* Tongue with a particular Grace and Beauty. Our language has received innumerable Elegancies and Improvements, from that Infusion of *Hebraisms*, which are derived to it out of the Poetical Passages in Holy Writ.

I think we should agree with the *Monthly Review*'s further dislike of the way Green changed metaphors into proper terms— e.g., 'Look graciously upon us' instead of 'Lift the light of thy countenance upon us':

> Many will be apt to think, that the spirit of the expression in these, and such like places, is very much flattened: and that the sense was sufficiently obvious before.

Some sensible rules were laid down by reviewers, who found the translators and revisers often sadly lacking in their practice. In 1789, the *Gentleman's Magazine*[2] says that biblical translators should avoid an affected diction:

> Moses should not be made to speak in a novel or foppish way.

[1] XXVIII (1763), 267–9.
[2] LIX (1789), 309.

The simplest terms should be made choice of; and the most obvious unadorned phrases, provided they are above vernacular vulgarity.

Obsolete, foreign, and learned words and phrases lead to obscurity. The *Magazine* quotes from Bishop Lowth. Where the Authorized Version says: 'They led them through the deep, as an horse, in the wilderness, that they should not stumble,' the bishop puts: 'Leading them through the abyss like a courser in the plain without obstacle.' As the *Magazine* says: 'How inflated the latter rendering, how purely English the former!' But neither is particularly clear.

It could be much worse. The prime example of how *not* to do it is the Liberal Version of the New Testament by Dr. Edward Harwood in 1768. True, it is a paraphrase and he had the best of intentions, but the effect is disastrous.

The *Monthly Review*[1] says well that Harwood wanted to make a polite version but lost simplicity. Whether *polite* here means polished or has its modern sense, I am not sure—elsewhere it was described as a version 'for gentlemen'.[2] The *Monthly* felt surprised that he should introduce more polished expressions than those of the old translation, for they 'rather degrade than add any real grace or dignity to the style and sentiments'. *Immolate* is no improvement on *sacrifice*: 'a certain opulent gentleman is not to be compared with 'a certain rich man'. Dr. Johnson lost all patience when he found that the simple 'Jesus wept' had become 'Jesus burst into a flood of tears'—so much so that he threw the book down, exclaiming, 'Puppy!'

And yet Harwood felt he was acting in the best interests of religion. He describes his work as an 'Attempt to translate the sacred writings with the same Freedom, Spirit and Elegance with which other English Translations from the Greek Classics have lately been executed'.[3] In his preface[4] he says he has put some years

[1] XXXVIII (1768), 217.
[2] G.M. LXIV (1794), 146.
[3] Title page.
[4] Preface, A 2.

of study to the work and has had the corrections of learned friends. He wants

> to Cloathe the genuine ideas and doctrines of the Apostles with that propriety and perspicuity in which they themselves . . . would have exhibited them had they *now* lived and written in our language.

His style suggests that they were all university philosophers, which may be all very well for St. Paul, but one wonders what St. Peter, the plain fisherman with an obvious accent, would have made of it.

For Harwood, the Authorized Version is 'bald and barbarous', but has acquired a 'venerable sacredness from length of time and custom', 'that every innovation of this capital nature would be generally stigmatized as the last and most daring enormity'.[1] Our language, he claims, has been so much refined of late that it now abounds in grace, purity, elegance, harmony, copiousness, and strength.[2] The trouble with Harwood's language is that it is so highly polished that you cannot get a grip on it. And yet he hoped[3] that his version might induce persons of 'liberal education and polite taste', and even the 'young and gay', to read the sacred volume. Here is the beginning of Harwood's version of the Parable of the Prodigal Son:

> A gentleman of a splendid family and opulent fortune had two sons. One day the younger approached his father, and begged him in the most importunate and soothing terms to make a partition of his effects betwixt himself and his elder brother. The indulgent father, overcome by his blandishments, immediately divided all his fortunes betwixt them.

Needless to say, the bluntness of the Authorized Version which tells how the young man 'would fain have filled his belly with the

[1] Ibid., p. v.
[2] Ibid., p. iv.
[3] Ibid., p. v.

husks that the swine did eat' is too much for Dr. Harwood—'he envied even the swine the husks which he saw them greedily devour—and would willingly have allayed with these the dire sensations he felt'.

If Harwood errs in one direction, William Williams, who published a harmony of the Gospels called *The Christian History*, erred in the opposite one. According to the *Critical Review*,[1] it was anything but elegant; rather it was low and familiar. Much of the phraseology which the *Review* disliked seems harmless enough now: 'the lad Jesus'; 'Zacharias was startled at the sight'; 'a great squall of wind'; 'They screamed out for fear'; 'They wanted to arrest him, but he escaped out of their clutches'.

Some of it is lively: e.g., the wicked servant in the parable who began 'to junket and carouse with sots', or the examples of bad language to your brother which Williams renders, 'whoever shall say to his brother Fie Skum—out Scoundrel'. Gilbert Wakefield thinks English has not words significant enough to render the force of the Hebrew words quoted in this passage, but Williams seems not to have done too badly.

'Vile, plebeian language,' says the *Critical*. But when I came to read Williams at some length I felt it was being unfair. If you pick out all the objectionable words and phrases and lay them end to end, it gives a wrong impression of their density. Some critics of the *New English Bible* strike me as having much of the spirit of the *Critical Review*.

There are also complaints about being too modern or too technical. Benjamin Blayney's version of *Jeremiah* and *Lamentations* was adversely criticized by the *Monthly*[2] in 1784 for using words like *regency, privy council, atoms, commanding officer, insulated, courier, inarticulately, annihilation*. 'It would be better to preserve accuracy by a *periphrasis*, than, in order scrupulously to maintain it, insert a word that is low or ludicrous, pedantic, or obscure.' They certainly sound more like a *Times* leader than Scripture.

Six years later, the *Critical Review*[3] attacked a version of the

[1] 43 (1777), 391–2.
[2] LXX (1784), 162.
[3] 69 (1790), 172.

Acts of the Apostles, by the Rev. John Willis, who preferred to call it *The Actions of the Apostles*. The reviewer stated that: 'It has been, and still continues to be, the opinion of many divines, that the style of the English version of the Holy Scriptures is uncouth, obsolete, and vulgar.' But Willis' version 'is confusion worse confounded—everything that can disgust and displease'. How could Mr. Willis think that 'to make an ejectment' was more likely to be understood than 'to lighten the ship', or that to make Claudius Lysias send *compliments* was better than to let him simply send *greetings*?

The *Review*[1] agreed that a new version was needed and was better pleased with Nathaniel Scarlett's New Testament which it considered in 1798. This, it said, used *immerse* for *baptise—dip* would have been preferable—but *denier* was better than *penny*, *taxgatherers* than *publicans*, *daemons* than *devils*; *blessed* was very properly at times changed to *happy*, *grace* to *favour*, *charity* to *love*.

As to these, we can still argue, like Tyndale, about *grace* and *favour*, *charity* and *love*. *Daemon* spelt with *ae* sounds no different from ordinary *demon*; and as for *denier*, it does not suggest false economies like *penny*, but it has been the name of too many coins, weights, and measures to be helpful. I suppose now *denier* suggests the weave of nylon stockings, which only shows that no man can foresee the associations which a later age will bring to his carefully-chosen words. I think we must have the denarius in default of a better word.

So far I have tried to outline a general picture of the activity in new versions of the Bible that went on all through the century, approaching some of them simply through the reviews, for I confess I have not read them all. I should now like to look in a little more detail at four middle-of-the-road and scholarly attempts. They are, in chronological order, Zachary Mudge's *Essay towards a New English Version of the Psalms from the Original Hebrew*, 1744; Thomas Percy's *The Song of Songs*, 1764; Robert Lowth's *New Translation* [of Isaiah] *with a Preliminary Dissertation and Notes*, 1788; and Gilbert Wakefield's translation of the *New Testament*, 1791. All these writers set out their scholarly

[1] New arr. XXIV (1798), 66.

principles, and it is to their credit that in some instances their alterations are confirmed by the renderings in *N.E.B.*

Mudge, Prebendary of Exeter and Vicar of St. Andrew's, Plymouth, says in his preface that the Psalms are not as well understood as they should be, but he makes no claim to set his version against the customary one. He offers it to the public for correction and improvement. He hopes that when the Wisdom of the Church thinks it time to authenticate a new translation of the Bible, his *Psalms* will make the task easier. Meanwhile, it may assist the private studies of readers. He proposes a plain, literal version without deviating into affected ornaments:

I have endeavour'd [he says] to express the Force of the Words; to preserve the Images; and, as I observed that generally best done in following the Hebrew Manner and Order of Composition, I have confirmed to it, as far as might be, the very structure of the sentence.

He notes that some Psalms would be clearer 'if we saw that they present different Scenes or States'; that punctuation is no authentic part of the text; that titles were generally added later; that David was not the author of all the Psalms.

Mudge makes few textual emendations; when he does, he says, it is usually with the concurrence of the Septuagint. But he does not prefer the readings of that version simply because it was the one quoted in the New Testament; that was mere accommodation to the custom of the times and does not make it a more authentic text.

It is clear that the wording and cadences of the Authorized Version are running in Mudge's head; he may alter moods and tenses, but he does not alter for alteration's sake. His version of the Shepherd Psalm will illustrate this. We may feel that *conducteth* is no improvement on *leadeth*, but at least it saves repetition. 'To length of days', I suppose, is his attempt to conform to Hebrew idiom, but it is less clear than the 'for ever' of the Authorized or the 'my whole life long' of *N.E.B.* Here is the whole Psalm:

The Lord is my shepherd; I shall not want. He causeth me to lie down in the Pastures of Herbage. He leads me beside the soft-flowing waters: He refresheth my soul; He conducteth me in the Paths of Righteousness. Even though I walked thro' the Valley of the Shadow of Death, I would not fear Evil; for thou wouldst be with me: thy Rod and thy Staff would comfort me; thou dressest out a Table in the Face of my Enemies; my Cup overfloweth. Doubtless Prosperity and Favour shall follow me all the Days of my life; and I shall sit in the House of the Lord to Length of Days.

In Psalm 90, the Authorized Version says: 'For all our days are passed away in thy wrath; we spend our years as a tale that is told.' Mudge puts 'our years are as a sigh', which is very close to N.E.B.'s 'our years die away like a murmur'.

Mudge's notes are interesting. In Ps. 42, v. 7, A.V. reads: 'Deep calleth unto deep, at the noise of thy waterspouts: all thy waves and thy billows are gone over me.' 'Everyone sees,' says Mudge, 'the common Translation to be forced.' He assumes the text to be corrupt and translates: 'Deep calleth unto deep with the noise of thy canals.' His note explains:

He expresses the Depth of his trouble by a Metaphor familiar to the Holy Writers. He considers himself as on the Bottom of an Ocean, overwhelmed by all its waves; when he hears one deep roaring to another, through subterraneous Canals or Caverns.

N.E.B. turns *waterspouts* into *cataracts*. Mudge's comment exemplifies the trouble any eighteenth-century text may give the modern reader. To our mind, a canal is a civilized invention, suggesting a man-made channel quite out of place in that context of natural forces. But as a geographical term, the word could then be used, like its twin *channel*, for any narrower piece of water connecting two larger ones. Presumably this is what Mudge had in mind. Equally disturbing to us are *satiate* with no idea of excess, *frolick* for much wilder pranks than it implies now, *sound out* meaning to praise rather than put out feelers. For example: 'Thou openest thy Hands and satiatest the Desire of every living thing,' where A.V.'s *satisfiest* strikes us as being well and good. The tone of *frolick* is perfectly clear when Mudge writes: 'Do not suffer my Heart to learn any evil Thing, to frolick wicked Frolicks with men that are Dealers in vanity.' In 'Praise the Lord, for it is good: sound out our God for it is cheerful,' the phrase is clear by context, but the A.V.'s 'sing praises' needs no context.

Thomas Percy's *Song of Solomon* makes the structure of the book much clearer than the A.V. does; he is as convinced as any modern that it is dramatic. He tells us in his preface that he has attempted

> to rescue one of the most beautiful pastorals in the world, as well as the most ancient, from that obscurity and confusion in which it has been involved by the injudicious practice of former commentators.

When we consider the long history of allegorical interpretation from the first century onwards by both Jewish and Christian scholars, and the few exceptions who took the book literally, we can see the common sense of Percy's remark that 'the generality [of commentators] have been so busily employed in opening or unfolding its allegorical meaning, as wholly to neglect that literal sense, which ought to be the basis of their discoveries'. He goes on to point out that the first duty of an expositor is to ascertain that lower and more obvious meaning. Otherwise all will be idle conjecture. 'It is,' he says, 'erecting an edifice without a foundation, which, however fair and goodly to the view, will be blown down by the slightest breath of true criticism.'

Percy holds that the allegory and the literal sense should be kept apart. He is inclined to believe that the book is allegorical, though his reasons are not irrefutable—the occurrence of such metaphors in spiritual senses, the age-old tradition, its presence in the Scriptures. But in his translation, Percy aims at giving only 'the plain, literal sense, to interpret it in a tolerably consistent manner, and to do some justice to the poetical beauties'.

Percy thinks the speakers are Solomon, the Spouse, her companions, and the Friends of the Bridegroom. Some critics, he records, have imagined a five-act drama, some a set of disconnected eclogues: it is not a regular drama constructed on Greek rules nor a set of unconnected pastorals, for it has the same speakers and theme throughout. He appends notes which show a wealth of learning about eastern customs and often justify his interpretation. He admits that the language is extravagant in places, but then, 'the Passions in their paroxisms are a kind of temporary madness'.

In the well-known passage when in A.V. the bride says: 'I am the rose of Sharon and the Lily of the Valleys', Percy argues that she isn't extolling herself, but comparing herself to a 'meer common wild flower'.

One of the most commonly quoted phrases, usually misapplied in a context of death, is 'until the day break and the shadows flee away'. It really occurs in a context of love and life. Percy anticipates N.E.B. by his 'until the day breathe', and in his note on the change he says: 'A local beauty. In those hot countries the dawn of day is attended with a fine refreshing breeze, much more grateful and desireable than the return of light itself.' N.E.B. says: 'When the day is cool . . .'.

Then there is that curious passage, which tells us, according to A.V., that Solomon made himself a chariot, which piece of equipment seems oddly out of place in a poem about love-making. Percy puts *bridal-bed* and notes that some have rendered it *chariot*, some *bed*:

> perhaps because it partook of the nature of both . . . a sort of moveable bed drawn or carried about in state, not unlike the Palanquins used in other parts of Asia, which answer at once with the purpose of rest and conveyance.

With *palanquin*, Percy has hit on the exact word chosen by the scholars of N.E.B.

In the Bride's lyrical description of the Beloved at the end of chapter V, the A.V. says: 'His mouth is most sweet.' Percy puts: 'His mouth is sweetness itself,' a near approach to N.E.B.'s: 'His whispers are sweetness itself.'

The Bride in A.V. invites the Beloved to go forth into the field and lodge in the villages, to get up early into the vineyards. 'There will I give thee my loves,' she says, adding that 'the mandrakes give a smell, and at our gate are all manner of pleasant fruits'. Percy puts *love* in the singular, which is surely more idiomatic, but he cannot believe in the mandrake—disagreeable, stinking plant that it is. We can only assume he had not looked at the quotation in Johnson's Dictionary which shows that the Mandrake was believed to be both a narcotic and a fertility drug. It was used to make love philtres, so, nasty or not, it is in place in the erotic context of the literal story.

Bishop Lowth's translation of *Isaiah* is dedicated to George III. It is 'an attempt to set in a just light the writings of the most sublime and elegant of the Prophets of the Old Testament' which he feels might merit the honour of 'his Majesty's gracious acceptance were the execution in any degree answerable to the design'.

You will recall that Lowth, as Professor of Poetry at Oxford, had lectured in Latin on the Sacred Poetry of the Hebrews, demonstrating that it was structurally based on what he called Parallelism—that special sense of this word is due to him. He was therefore justified in claiming that the manner and form of the book had never been thought of, let alone attempted by any translator, ancient or modern.

The essential point missed by previous translators is, of course, that much of *Isaiah* is poetry, not prose, and Lowth's version makes a clear distinction between the two modes of composition in the same way as modern versions do. He holds that English has assimilated Hebrew modes of expression to its own benefit. He does not alter A.V. unless he feels it necessary, for 'the style of that translation is not only excellent in itself, but has taken possession of our ear, and of our taste'.

Also, he sees that any later literal translation must 'tread in the footsteps' of its predecessor:

The most obvious, the properest, and perhaps the only terms which the language affords are already occupied; and without going out of his way to find worse [the translator] cannot avoid them.

The style of A.V. admits of no improvement, but there are num-
berless improvements that need to be made as knowledge advan-
ces. In chapter 52, v. 15, A.V. says: 'So shall he sprinkle many
nations.' Despite the use of the phrase in a hymn which congrega-
tions still sing, one cannot help wondering what it means. Lowth
says the Hebrew is unsatisfactory grammatically: he renders it:
'So many nations shall look on him with admiration,' and if we
remember that in Lowth's period *admiration* could still have an
element of awe in it, this is not far from *N.E.B.* which reads:
'So many nations recoil at sight of him.' Again: 'They shall mount
up with wings as eagles' in chapter 40 appears in Lowth as: 'They
shall put forth fresh feathers like the moulting eagle,' which agrees
with the 'grow wings' of *N.E.B.* In the passage in chapter 3 which
catalogues female finery and must be the despair of all translators,
Lowth, like *N.E.B.*, opts for *turbans* instead of A.V.'s *hoods* in
v. 23; it sounds more oriental.

I quote part of chapter 35 to give some idea of Lowth's general
method:

> In the wilderness shall burst forth waters,
> And torrents in the desert;
> And the glowing sand shall become a pool,
> And the thirsty soil bubbling springs,
> And in the haunt of dragons shall spring forth
> The grass, with the reed and the bulrush,
> And a high-way shall be there—
> And it shall be called the way of holiness:
> No unclean person shall pass through it,
> But He himself shall be with them, walking in the way,
> And the foolish shall not err therein.

That may not be in complete accord with modern scholarship,
but at least it flows smoothly and makes sense.

Gilbert Wakefield issued his New Testament in 1791. He was a
Cambridge scholar of alleged Unitarian leanings, though the
Cambridge History of the Bible itself says that no sectarianism appears
in this translation. But he himself says he is aware that some
passages will please neither the orthodox nor the Socinian. He

keeps closely to the A.V., making changes in the interests of accuracy or modern usage. The critics said the result was a 'motley' style.

The 'wise men from the East' become *magi*; 'fruits meet for repentance' become *suitable*; 'tempted of the devil' becomes 'tried by the devil'; the old-fashioned phrase 'he was afterward an hungered' becomes 'at last he was hungry'. Throughout the Beatitudes he uses *happy* for *blessed*. Usually he prefers *teacher* to *prophet*, *taxgathers* to *publicans*. The *mote* in the eye is a *splinter*. Where the disciples on the stormy lake cry out in A.V., 'Save, Lord, we perish,' Wakefield puts, 'Master, save us! We are lost,' which in the state of their faith at the time sounds more natural. 'The fowls of the air have nests' becomes 'the birds of the air have roosts', which anticipates *N.E.B.* Surprisingly, Judas is said to have been 'choked with anguish' instead of having hanged himself; Wakefield justifies his rendering in a textual note. He tends to adjust weights and measures to English standards—involving firkins and furlongs.

His rendering of the Prodigal Son passage keeps fairly close to A.V. His prodigal indulges in *disorderly* living; 'the husks that the swine did eat' becomes 'the offal that the swine were eating'. He brings out the elder brother's querulous tone by putting: 'Thou never gavest me *even* a kid,' instead of leaving it to the reader's tone of voice to make plain. The opening verses of St. John's Gospel appear in Wakefield like this:

In the beginning was wisdom, and wisdom was with God and wisdom was God. The same was in the beginning with God. All things were made by it, and without it was nothing made. What was made had life in it, and this life was the light of man: and this light shineth in darkness, and the darkness hindered it not.

Wakefield's preface argues that 'learned and ingenious men of all persuasions have agreed on the wisdom' of making an amended version of the Scriptures. He admits that others oppose it as needless and dangerous, but, distinguished as they are, he does not see that they have 'any reputation for theological pursuits'. I have sometimes thought that this also happens now.

He states the rule he has tried to follow—to adopt the received version upon all possible occasions. The impossible occasions are when the words are low, obsolete, or obscure, the idiom vulgar, the phrase coarse, or uncouth, the construction intricate, the combination of terms harsh, the sense misrepresented. Then he tries to make the translation as completely vernacular as he can, without vulgarity, so that it shall be a specimen 'of pure, unaffected English diction', and he pleads for the use of the native element rather than the Latin.

With a palpable hit at Dr. Harwood, Wakefield declares:

> What are called *liberal translations* of the Scriptures, I never could approve; considering them as too much calculated to weaken the dignity and efficacy of the sacred writings and expose them to ridicule and contempt.

To him it seems 'a most ignoble ambition to court the sickly tastes of those readers, to whom the natural plainness of the gospel has no relish'.

These new translations, paraphrases, and revisions that I have asked you to consider are only a sample; but I hope they may have proved of some interest in the year that has seen the publication of the complete *N.E.B.* One wonders what these eighteenth-century scholars would think of it—whether they would see it as the fulfilment of their hopes, or, shaking their heads over the decline of English, find it too colloquial, stilted, or uncertain in tone. If they dealt out adverse criticism, it would be no more than they dealt out to each other in their pursuit of that unattainable perfect vision which is always over the horizon.

The Publications of Beatrice M. I. White

To save space, one recurrent item is deliberately omitted: Professor White's editorial work for *The Year's Work in English Studies*, from 1952 to 1955 as co-editor of volumes XXXI–XXXIV (1950–53), and from 1956 to 1965 as editor of volumes XXXV–XLIV (1954–63).

E & S *Essays and Studies*

E.E.T.S. *The Early English Text Society*

MLR *The Modern Language Review*

NM *Neuphilologische Mitteilungen*

NR *The National Review*

RES *The Review of English Studies*

YWES *The Year's Work in English Studies*

1927
'The Three Editions of the Dialogue: A Collation', in *The Dialogue Concerning Tyndale by Sir Thomas More Reproduced in Black Letter Facsimile*, edd. W. E. Campbell and A. W. Reed (Eyre & Spottiswoode).

1928
The Eclogues of Alexander Barclay (E.E.T.S., no. 175).
Analytical Index and Table of Chapter Contents in *The Intelligent Woman's Guide to Socialism and Capitalism*, George Bernard Shaw (Constable).

1931
The Dance of Death, John Lydgate (E.E.T.S., no. 181) (completing Florence Warren's transcripts and collations).
A Dialogue Concerning Witches and Witchcraftes 1593, George Gifford (Shakespeare Association Facsimiles, no. 1, O.U.P.).
'Notes: Three Rare Books about Women', *Huntington Library Bulletin*.
'Two Tracts on Marriage by Robert Copland', *Huntington Library Bulletin*.
'A Note on Alexander Barclay', *MLR* XXVI.

1932
The Vulgaria of John Stanbridge and the Vulgaria of Robert Whittinton (E.E.T.S., no. 187).
'The Talkies and English Speech', *American Speech* VII.

1933
Royal Nonesuch: A Tudor Tapestry (Jonathan Cape).

1934
An Index to 'The Elizabethan Stage' and 'William Shakespeare: A Study of Facts and Problems' by Sir Edmund Chambers (O.U.P.).

1935
Mary Tudor (Macmillan).
'An Early Tudor Grammarian' [Robert Whittinton], *MLR* XXX.

1936
'Murder in the Tower', *NR* CVII.
Review of *Lord Burghley in Shakespeare*, G. W. Phillips (Thornton Butterworth), *NR* CVII.

1937
Review of *The Life and Death of Robert Devereux, Earl of Essex*, G. B. Harrison (Cassell, 1937), *NR* CVIII.

1938
Reviews of *Shakespeare's Vital Secret*, R. M. Lucas (Rydal Press, 1937), *Shakespeare's Last Plays*, E. M. W. Tillyard (Chatto & Windus, 1938), and *In Shakespeare's Warwickshire and the Unknown Years*, Oliver Baker (Simpkin, 1937), *NR* CX.

1939
'King Christian IV in England', *NR* CXII.

1940
'There Were Traitors Then', *NR* CXV.
Contributor of the section 'Alexander Barclay' in *The Cambridge Bibliography of English Literature*, ed. F. W. Bateson (C.U.P.).

1941
'That Other Armada', *NR* CXVI.
'Torture Then and Now', *NR* CXVII.

1942
'The Restoration', *YWES* XXI (1940).

1944
'The Restoration', *YWES* XXII (1941).
'The Restoration', *YWES* XXIII (1942).
Review of *A Dictionary of American English on Historical Principles: Part XIII*, edd. Sir William Craigie and James R. Hulbert (Univ. of Chicago Press and O.U.P., 1942), *RES* XX.

1945
'Mary Coleridge: An Appreciation', *E & S* XXXI.
'The Restoration', *YWES* XXIV (1943).
'Three Notes on Old and Middle English: Whale-Hunting; The Barnacle Goose; and the Date of the Ancrene Riwle', *MLR* XL.
'"Chevisaunce" as a Flower Name', *RES* XXI.

1946
Review of *Virginia Woolf: Her Art as a Novelist*, Joan Bennett (C.U.P., 1945), *MLR* XLI.

Review of *English Literature at the Close of the Middle Ages*, E. K. Chambers (Clarendon Press, 1945), *MLR* XLI.

Review of *Verbal Repetition in the 'Ancrene Riwle'*, Sister Agnes Margaret Humbert (Catholic Univ. of America Press, 1944), *RES* XXII.

Review of *A Dictionary of American English on Historical Principles: Parts XIV–XX*, edd. Sir William Craigie and James R. Hulbert (Univ. of Chicago Press and O.U.P., 1944), *RES* XXII.

Review of *American Speech: A Quarterly of Linguistic Usage*, Vol. XVIII, No. 2–Vol. XX, No. 3 (Columbia Univ. Press, 1943–5), *RES* XXII.

1948

Review of *Gautier Map, Conteur Anglais. Extraits du 'De Nugis Curialium'*, A. Boutemy (Brussels: Collection Lebègue, 1945), *MLR* XLIII.

Review of *Sire Gauvain et le Chevalier Vert*, E. Pons (Paris: Aubier, 1946), *MLR* XLIII.

1949

Review of *The Cloud of Unknowing and The Book of Privy Counselling*, ed. Phyllis Hodgson (E.E.T.S. no. 218, 1944), *MLR* XLIV.

Review of *The Good Wife Taught her Daughter; The Good Wyfe Wold a Pylgremage; The Thewis of Gud Women*, ed. Tauno F. Mustanoja (Helsinki: Annales Academiae Scientiarum Fennicae B. LXI, 1948), *MLR* XLIV.

Review of *The Plantagenets, 1154–1485*, John Harvey (Batsford, 1948), *MLR* XLIV.

Review of *Medieval English Verse and Prose in Modernized Versions*, R. S. Loomis and Rudolph Willard (Appleton–Century–Crofts, 1948), *MLR* XLIV.

1950

'Fact and Fancy in Medieval English Literature', *Essays by Divers Hands* XXV.

Review of *The Harley Lyrics: The Middle English Lyrics of MS. Harley 2253*, ed. G. L. Brook (Manchester Univ. Press, 1948), *RES* n.s.I.

1952

'Frederick James Furnivall', *E & S* n.s.V.

'The Nineteenth Century and After I' [Books], *YWES* XXXI (1950).

Review of *The Romance of Sir Degrevant*, ed. L. F. Casson (E.E.T.S. no. 221,1949), *MLR* XLVII.

Reviews of *Skelton. The Life and Times of an Early Tudor Poet*, H. L. R. Edwards (Jonathan Cape, 1949) and *John Skelton. A Selection from his Poems*, ed. Vivian de Sola Pinto (Sidgwick & Jackson, 1950), *RES* n.s. III.

1953

'Two Notes on Middle English: Chaucer's "camail" and "aventail" [*Clerk's Tale* 1195 f.]; *Sir Gawain and the Green Knight*, l. 295 [*barlay*]', *Neophilologus* XXXVII.

'The Nineteenth Century and After I' [Books], *YWES* XXXII (1951).

Review of *A Dictionary of Americanisms on Historical Principles*, ed. Mitford M. Mathews (Univ. of Chicago Press and O.U.P., 1951), *RES* n.s. IV.

1954
'Medieval Animal Lore', *Anglia* LXXII.
'Middle English I. Chaucer', *YWES* XXXIII (1952).
Review of *William Barnes, Linguist*, Willis D. Jacobs (Univ. of New Mexico Press, 1952), *RES* n.s. V.

1955
'The Teaching of Literature', *English* X.

1957
Review of *A talkyng of þe loue of God*, ed. C. M. Westra ('S–Gravenhage: M. Nijhoff, 1950), *Medium Ævum* XXVI.
Review of *The Life of Saint George*, Alexander Barclay (ed. William Nelson) (E.E.T.S. no. 230, 1955), *RES* n.s. VIII.

1959
'Claudius and Fortune', *Anglia* LXXVII.

1960
'Medieval Mirth', *Anglia* LXXVIII.
Review of *Þe Wohunge of Ure Lauerd*, ed. W. Meredith Thompson (E.E.T.S. no. 241, 1958), *Speculum* XXXV.

1961
'Ultima Thule: Some English Travellers to Iceland', *E & S* n.s. XIV.
'Traditional Animal Lore: The Beast Book in Medical History', *St. Mary's Hospital Gazette* LXVII.

1962
Collector, *Essays and Studies* n.s. XV (John Murray).

1963
'Two Chaucer Notes: 1. Proper Names in the *Canterbury Tales*; 2. A "Minced" Oath in *Sir Thopas*', *NM* LXIV.
'Decline and Fall of Interjections', *NM* LXIV.

1964
'Two Notes on "Hamlet": Hamlet's Reading; Hamlet's "Bold Bawdry"', *NM* LXV.

1965
Cast of Ravens: The Strange Case of Sir Thomas Overbury (London: John Murray; New York: George Braziller).
'Medieval Beasts', *E & S* n.s. XVIII.
'The Green Knight's Classical Forebears', *NM* LXVI.

1966
'Of Ghosts and Spirits Walking by Day and by Night', *Studies in Language and Literature in Honour of Margaret Schlauch*, edd. M. Brahmer, S. Helsztyński, and J. Krzyżanowski (Warsaw: Polish Scientific Publishers).

1967
Philobiblon: The Love of Books in Life and in Literature (The Library Association. Arundell Esdaile Memorial Lecture, 1966).

1968
'The Elusive Boundaries of "Terra Ridentium"', *Chaucer und Seine Zeit: Symposion für Walter F. Schirmer*, ed. Arno Esch (Tübingen: Max Niemeyer).

1969
'Saracens and Crusaders: from Fact to Allegory', *Medieval Literature and Civilization: Studies in Memory of G. N. Garmonsway*, edd. D. A. Pearsall and R. A. Waldron (The Athlone Press).

1971
'Poet and Peasant', *The Reign of Richard II: Essays in Honour of May McKisack*, edd. F. R. H. du Boulay and Caroline M. Barron (The Athlone Press).

Forthcoming
'Cain's Kin', *The Witch Figure: Essays in Honour of Dr. K. M. Briggs*, ed. Venetia Newall (Routledge & Kegan Paul).
'A Persistent Paradox', *Folklore*.

C.G.H.